ARRIVALS

CROSS-CULTURAL EXPERIENCES IN LITERATURE

Jann Huizenga

College of Santa Fe

Addison-Wesley Publishing Company
Reading, Massachusetts • Menlo Park, California
New York • Don Mills, Ontario • Wokingham, England
Amsterdam • Bonn • Sydney • Singapore • Tokyo
Madrid • San Juan • Paris • Seoul, Korea • Milan
Mexico City • Taipei, Taiwan

Arrivals: Cross-Cultural Experiences in Literature

Copyright © 1995 by Addison-Wesley Publishing Company, Inc.
All rights reserved.
No part of this publication may be reproduced,
stored in a retrieval system, or transmitted
in any form or by any means, electronic, mechanical,
photocopying, recording, or otherwise,
without the prior permission of the publisher.

Text and Photo credits: Credits appear on pages 185–187.

A publication of World Language Division
Editorial director: Joanne Dresner
Acquisitions editor: Allen Ascher
Development editor: Françoise Leffler
Production editor: Liza Pleva
Text design: The Wheetley Company, Inc.
Text design adaptation: Circa 86
Cover design: Joseph DePinho
Cover illustration/photo: © James Staff
Art research: Curt Belshe

Library of Congress Cataloging-in-Publication Data

Arrivals : cross-cultural experiences in literature / [selected by]
  Jann Huizenga.
      p.   cm.
   Includes index
   ISBN 0-201-82530-9
   1. English language—Textbooks for foreign speakers.   2. Pluralism
(Social sciences)—Problems, exercises, etc.   3. Minorities—United
States—Problems, exercises, etc.   4. Readers—Pluralism (Social
sciences).   5. Readers—Minorities.   I. Huizenga, Jann.
PE1128.A683   1995
428.6'4—dc20   94-30093
                                                        CIP

1 2 3 4 5 6 7 8 9 10-CRS-98979695

To Kim,
for nurturing this
in so many ways.

And to my family and friends,
for just being there.

CONTENTS

TO THE TEACHER

Arrivals contains eighteen short stories, poems, and excerpts from novels and memoirs, all written in English by first– or second–generation immigrants or visitors to North America. All the authors are professional writers who have, for the most part, gathered awards, honors, and critical acclaim for their writing. Each piece deals with some aspect of the cross-cultural experience in North America and was selected for its accessibility and potential to captivate ESL readers.

Though *Arrivals* focuses on developing reading skills and strategies, the activities built around the literary selections carefully integrate writing, speaking, and listening as well.

Intended Audience

Arrivals is appropriate for young adult and adult students of ESL at an intermediate to advanced reading level. It is especially recommended for students in credit or noncredit college and university ESL programs. Good readers in an upper-level ABE or high school program will also enjoy it.

Goals

Arrivals aims to do the following:

1. **Develop overall language and communication ability.** At every stage, reading is integrated with writing, speaking, and listening. Vocabulary development and grammar work also play a role.

2. **Foster the type of academic literacy necessary for North American contexts.** Successful readers need to do much more than retrieve information from a text, and *Arrivals* seeks to promote this awareness. Tasks encourage interactive reading: comparing what one reads with one's personal experience, evaluating it, expressing opinions about it, and so on. By encouraging students to do much more than find or recall information from texts, *Arrivals* attempts to counter the passive reading styles that many students have grown accustomed to. It promotes higher-order thinking skills essential for successful academic and professional performance in North America and elsewhere.

3. **Develop good reading strategies.** *Arrivals* trains readers in the use of strategies through a two-layered approach. First, its activities model strategic, text-appropriate approaches at the stages of pre-reading, while-reading, and post-reading. Second, small boxes flag particular reading strategies that are called for in certain activities, making the strategies available to students in a very explicit way. Students are also asked to reflect on specific strategies and evaluate their effectiveness for them personally. This holistic, strategy-oriented training develops independent readers, who acquire a repertoire of strategies for future use.

4. **Help students discover literature and how their lives are reflected in it.** In terms of introducing students to the art of literature, the text reflects a pedagogy of discovery. Activities lead students to discover literary tensions or dichotomies, imagery, symbolism, and other literary and stylistic devices.

5. **Encourage students to think critically.** They are repeatedly called upon to analyze, compare, evaluate, give opinions, and so on. Each unit ends with a Review section, which requires students to find similarities across texts or to evaluate one in light of the others.

6. **Develop an interactive community of readers.** In real life, we respond personally to what we read, discussing it with others and making it an integral part of our social and professional communication. This allows us to clarify our thoughts on various issues and encourages us to continue reading. *Arrivals* provides numerous opportunities for reader response and peer interaction, which is vital to readers' growth and motivation.

Organization and Activities

Arrivals contains six thematic units, most of which have three lessons centering on the topic at hand. In-depth reading, where students read several texts on the same theme, lightens the cognitive load for readers by providing a predictable framework. Students can build on what has come before as they progress through a unit. The authentic texts are further made accessible by the fact that their contents—themes of cross-cultural adjustment, homesickness, language learning, and so on—are so familiar to ESL readers. Additionally, the design and step-by-step sequencing of the activities in each lesson—which progress from previewing to global reading to focused reading and then to analyzing—go a long way toward ensuring comprehension.

In each lesson, students can expect the same organization. **Anticipate the Story** provides a very general overview for readers, gets them to call on their own related background knowledge, has them write questions they would like answered, and encourages readers in other ways to predict what they might read.

Global Reading encourages students to read the text through for the gist. Students read globally to see if they can find answers to questions they wrote, to answer a general question posed in the text, or simply to capture what they think are the main ideas of the text. At this point, students always write a short reaction, **Reader Response,** which they share with a partner or group. Peer sharing of initial reactions and main ideas at this point prepares the way for finer-tuned reading at the next stage.

While space is provided in the text itself for the written reaction, you may prefer for students to buy a separate notebook, not only to record these responses, but to record later reactions to and comments on the stories, in the fashion of a dialogue journal. You could collect these journals at intervals, commenting on their contents, or you could ask students periodically to read some favorite entries to a partner, group, or the class.

Focused Reading provides students with a chart, graph, or other device to structure their reading while at the same time allowing them to discover the importance of details in the story. After sharing their discoveries with others in the class, they are ready to move on to an analysis of the text. This section would be ideal for homework, if you have limited time for in-class reading.

Analyze the Story is set up as a small-group discussion. Groups can choose one of three options to discuss and reach a conclusion about. Giving groups a time limit of ten minutes or so to discuss and prepare their "reportback" will help them focus on the task and work diligently. The questions in this section can also be dealt with in whole-class discussions, if you prefer. If time allows, groups can be assigned all three questions to discuss.

Look at Language deals with language on a variety of levels. It is also an ideal homework assignment. In this section students work on guessing the meaning of new words from context, vocabulary development (idioms, word forms, domains), literary devices, and grammatical patterns.

Move Beyond the Story offers ideas for related and extended discussion and writing. Students are encouraged to relate what they have read to their own personal lives and to the wider world. Tasks here are varied and lively, and range from doing surveys and questionnaires to writing real letters to the authors of the literary pieces. Students can choose one task from among the three or four given, or you can ask them to choose one for discussion and one for writing. The writing tasks would be most successful if they were followed up by peer reading and response and otherwise dealt with in a process-oriented approach.

ACKNOWLEDGMENTS

I'd like to thank the many friends and colleagues who helped shape this book. Nancy Gross, at LaGuardia Community College, CUNY, reviewed and field-tested the material and gave me invaluable feedback and encouragement, as did her students. Maria Thomas-Ruzic, my coauthor on other projects, helped develop and clarify my thoughts on teaching reading in the long discussions we had, as did my graduate students at the College of Santa Fe. Reviewers Howard Sage, American Language Institute at New York University, Laura Le Dréan, English Language Institute at the University of Houston-Downtown, and Tere Ross, American Language Institute at California State University-Long Beach, provided crucial and constructive criticism that led to numerous revisions in the second draft of the manuscript. Wendy Watkins's help with permissions, photos, author biodata, and activities in the final stages saved the day. At Addison-Wesley World Language, editorial director Joanne Dresner and editors Allen Ascher, Françoise Leffler, Lynne Telson Barsky, and Liza Pleva provided constant guidance, fine attention to detail, and other much-much-appreciated expertise. Thanks also to Laura McCormick for tracking down some hard-to-get permissions. I'm grateful to the writers included here, not only for their willingness to contribute to this anthology, but for the photos, suggestions, and encouragement many provided. Finally, many thanks to my wonderful family and especially my husband, Kim, whose imprint is evident throughout the book.

ARRIVALS

CROSS-CULTURAL
EXPERIENCES
IN LITERATURE

Arriving

The three texts in this unit are about arriving in North America. What were your impressions, reactions, or feelings when you first arrived here? What was new or strange? What was disappointing? What was fun or exciting? Write about one or more of these questions in your journal.

1

Meet the Author

EVA HOFFMAN *(born 1945)*

EVA HOFFMAN was born in Krakow, Poland. When she was thirteen, she immigrated with her family to Vancouver, Canada. She studied English and American literature at Harvard University. The following excerpt is taken from her autobiographical book *Lost in Translation* (1989). It is a beautiful account of her journey to a new world and into a new language. The book also provides a European perspective on North American life.

Ms. Hoffman lives in New York City.

1. Anticipate the Story

In the following excerpt from her memoir, *Lost in Translation,* the author tells about her arrival in Canada from Poland at the age of thirteen. She describes her family's long train trip from Montreal to Vancouver, their final destination.

Find Poland on the map on page 181, and then trace the author's route on this map of Canada.

Preview the text by looking at the title and reading the first sentence of each paragraph. What general information do you learn about the trip?

2. Global Reading

Read the text through to get the general idea. Was young Eva's arrival in North America anything like yours?

Jot down your reactions or questions about the passage here or in your journal. Then share them with a partner or group.

This is what one student wrote:

> **READING STRATEGY**
>
> Before reading, get some general information about a text. Look at the title, any subtitles, and any pictures. You can also read the first sentence of each paragraph. This is called *previewing.*

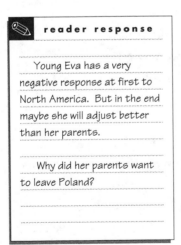

reader response

Young Eva has a very negative response at first to North America. But in the end maybe she will adjust better than her parents.

Why did her parents want to leave Poland?

reader response

Exile

◆◆

Eva Hoffman

WE ARE IN MONTREAL, in an echoing, dark train station, and we are huddled on a bench waiting for someone to give us some guidance. Timidly, I walk a few steps away from my parents to explore this terra incognita,° and I come back with snippets° of amazing news. There is this young girl, maybe my age, in high-heeled shoes and lipstick! She looks so vulgar,° I complain. Or maybe this is just some sort of costume? There is also a black man at whom I stare for a while; he's as handsome as Harry Belafonte,* the only black man whose face I know from pictures in Polish magazines, except here he is, big as life. Are all black men this handsome, I wonder?

terra incognita: new, unknown place

snippets: bits or pieces

vulgar: common; lacking refinement

2   Eventually, a man speaking broken Polish approaches us, takes us to the ticket window, and then helps us board our train. And so begins yet another segment of this longest journey—all the longer because we don't exactly know when it will end, when we'll reach our destination. We only know that Vancouver is very far away.

3   The people on the train look at us askance,° and avoid sitting close to us. This may be because we've brought suitcases full of dried cake, canned sardines, and sausages, which would keep during the long transatlantic journey. We don't know about dining cars, and when we discover that this train has such a thing, we can hardly afford to go there once a day on the few dollars that my father has brought with him. Two dollars could buy a bicycle, or several pairs of shoes in Poland. It seems like a great deal to pay for four bowls of soup.

look at us askance: look at us indirectly and disapprovingly

4   The train cuts through endless expanses of terrain, most of it flat and monotonous,° and it seems to me that the relentless rhythm of the wheels is like scissors cutting a three-thousand-mile rip through my life. From now on, my life will be divided into two parts, with the line drawn by that train. After a while, I subside into a silent indifference,° and I don't want to look at the landscape anymore; these are not the friendly fields, the farmyards of Polish countryside; this is vast,° dull, and formless. By the time we reach the Rockies,° my parents try to pull me

monotonous: unchanging

indifference: lack of interest or feeling

vast: huge

Rockies: Rocky Mountains

---

*An American singer popular in the 1950s and 60s.

out of my stupor° and make me look at the spectacular landscapes we're passing by. But I don't want to. These peaks° and ravines, these mountain streams and enormous boulders° hurt my eyes—they hurt my soul. They're too big, too forbidding,° and I can't imagine feeling that I'm part of them, that I'm in them. I recede into sleep; I sleep through the day and the night, and my parents can't shake me out of it. My sister, perhaps recoiling° even more deeply from all this strangeness, is in a state of feverish illness and can hardly raise her head.

5   On the second day, we briefly meet a passenger who speaks Yiddish. My father enters into an animated conversation with him and learns some thrilling tales. For example, there's the story of a Polish Jew who came to Canada and made a fortune—he's now a millionaire!—on producing Polish pickles.° Pickles! If one can make a fortune on that, well—it shouldn't be hard to get rich in this country. My father is energized, excited by this story, but I subside into an even more determined sullenness.° "Millionaire" is one of those fairy-tale words that has no meaning to me whatsoever—a word like "emigration" or "Canada." In spite of my parents' protestations,° I go back to sleep, and I miss some of the most prized sights on the North American continent.

▪ ▪ ▪

6   By the time we've reached Vancouver, there are very few people left on the train. My mother has dressed my sister and me in our best outfits—identical navy blue dresses with sailor collars and gray coats handmade of good gabardine. My parents' faces reflect anticipation and anxiety. "Get off the train on the right foot," my mother tells us. "For luck in the new life."

7   I look out of the train window with a heavy heart. Where have I been brought to? As the train approaches the station, I see what is indeed a bit of nowhere. It's a drizzly° day, and the platform is nearly empty. Everything is the color of slate.° From this bleakness,° two figures approach us—a nondescript middle-aged man and woman—and after making sure that we are the right people, the arrivals from the other side of the world, they hug us; but I don't feel much warmth in their half-embarrassed embrace.° "You should kneel down and kiss the ground," the man tells my parents. "You're lucky to be here." My parents' faces fill with a kind of naïve° hope. Perhaps everything will be well after all. They need signs, portents,° at this hour.

8   Then we get into an enormous° car—yes, this is America—and drive into the city that is to be our home. ◆

stupor: a dulled state of mind

peaks: mountain tops

boulders: large rocks

forbidding: dangerous or frightening

recoiling: drawing away from

pickles: cucumbers preserved in vinegar

sullenness: silent, angry, unsociable behavior

protestations: objections

drizzly: lightly rainy

slate: a gray stone

bleakness: a cheerless, harsh situation

embrace: hug

naïve: innocent, childlike

portents: signs that something is going to happen

enormous: huge

3. Focused Reading

As you reread the story, fill in this chart. Write down words the author uses to describe the new people, places, and stories young Eva is exposed to. Then choose adjectives from the list to describe how Eva feels about them.

New People, Places, and Stories	Words She Uses To Describe Them	How She Feels About Them
young girl in Montreal	vulgar	shocked + maybe disgusted
black man in Montreal		
flat landscape		
Rocky Mountains		
story of Polish millionaire		
Vancouver		

ADJECTIVES
angry
bored
depressed
disgusted
excited
indifferent
interested
pained
pleasantly surprised
shocked

Discuss your chart with a partner. Are any of Eva's reactions similar to those you had on arrival here?

4. Analyze the Story

In groups, choose one of the following to discuss. Elect a group member to report your conclusions to the class.

A. Do Eva's parents and sister feel the way she does about arriving in North America? How are their reactions similar to or different from Eva's reactions?

B. In the last paragraph, young Eva identifies the "enormous car" with her idea of America. What do you think she means?

C. The author doesn't discuss Poland much in this text, but we can draw conclusions or *infer* certain things about the life and home she left behind. List three to five *inferences* you can make about Eva's former life.

5. Look at Language

A. *Study the nouns in bold in these sentences from the text. What do they have in common? How are the nouns formed?*

> My sister, perhaps recoiling even more deeply from all this **strangeness**, is in a state of feverish **illness** and can hardly raise her head. (paragraph 4)

> My father is energized, excited by this story, but I subside into an even more determined **sullenness**. (paragraph 5)

> It's a drizzly day, and the platform is nearly empty. Everything is the color of slate. From this **bleakness**, two figures approach us. . . . (paragraph 7)

All of the above nouns were formed by adding the suffix **-ness** to an adjective (**strange, ill, sullen, bleak**).

Now make nouns from these adjectives in the same way.

sad	*sadness*	empty	
happy	*happiness*	full	
soft		sweet	
hard		bitter	

B. *Now study the nouns in bold below. How are they formed?*

> "Millionaire" is one of those fairy-tale words that has no meaning to me whatsoever—a word like "**emigration**" or "Canada." In spite of my parents' **protestations**, I go back to sleep. . . . (paragraph 5)

> My parents' faces reflect **anticipation** and anxiety. (paragraph 6)

The above nouns were formed by adding the suffix **-ion** (with some spelling modifications) to a verb (**emigrate, protest, anticipate**).

Now make nouns from these verbs in the same way.

attract ___attraction___   connect _____

create ___creation___   act _____

operate _____   direct _____

collect _____   legislate _____

prevent _____   elect _____

6. Move Beyond the Story

Discussion

Young Eva traveled all the way across the North American continent and, when she wasn't escaping into sleep, saw many different places and landscapes. What places have you seen or visited in North America? Share your favorite place with a small group. Take notes on the information your classmates give you.

Favorite Place in North America	Exact Location	Reasons Why It's Great

Writing

A. In paragraph 7, the author describes her first impressions of her new home, Vancouver. She paints a sad and gray picture with the following words and phrases:

heavy heart	a bit of nowhere
drizzly day	nearly empty
color of slate	bleakness
nondescript	half-embarrassed embrace

Paint a picture with words of your first impression of North America (or another place you have been).

B. Write about a time in your youth when you felt like Eva: angry, sullen, or sad.

Meet the Author

OSCAR HIJUELOS *(born 1951)*

OSCAR HIJUELOS was born to Cuban immigrant parents in New
York City. He was educated at City College of New York. In 1990, at
the age of thirty-eight, Mr. Hijuelos became the first Hispanic
American to win the Pulitzer Prize for Fiction for his novel *The
Mambo Kings Play Songs of Love*. The following excerpt comes
from his first novel, *Our House in the Last World* (1983), which tells
the story of a Cuban immigrant family in the United States.

Mr. Hijuelos lives in New York City, in the same Upper West Side
neighborhood where he grew up.

1. Anticipate the Story

The following passage is from the novel *Our House in the Last World*. The novel tells the story of the Santinio family (Alejo, Mercedes, and their sons, Hector and Horacio), who came from Cuba to New York City searching for a better life. In this passage, relatives from Cuba arrive at the Santinio home.

Find Cuba on the map on page 180. Exchange information with classmates about Cuba. Why have so many Cubans immigrated to the United States? Write your ideas down here.

_____

_____

_____

_____

_____

> **READING STRATEGIES**
>
> Good readers don't stop when they see a new word. They read on to see if the context will give some clues to meaning.

2. Global Reading

Read the story as quickly as you can to get the main idea. Don't use your dictionary. Try to understand some of the new words from the context, the words or sentences that come before or after an unfamiliar word.

Jot down your reactions or questions about the story here or in your journal. Share them with a partner or group.

> **HOW YOU READ**
>
> Which new words could you understand from the context?

reader response

Visitors, 1965

◆◆

Oscar Hijuelos

IT WAS LATE NIGHT when a van pulled up to the building and its four exhausted° passengers stepped onto the sidewalk. Seeing the arrival from the window, Mercedes was in a trance° for a moment and then removed her apron and ran out, almost falling down the front steps, waving her arms and calling, "Aaaaiiii, aaaaiiii, aaaaiiii! Oh my God! My God! My God," and giving many kisses. Alejo followed and hugged Pedro. The female cousins waited humbly, and then they began kissing Mercedes and Alejo and Hector and Horacio, their hats coming off and teeth chattering and hair getting all snarled like ivy on an old church . . . kisses, kisses, kisses . . . into the warm lobby with its deep, endless mirrors and the mailbox marked *Delgado/Santinio.* The female cousins, like china dolls, were incredibly beautiful, but were struck dumb by the snow and the new world, silent because there was something dreary° about the surroundings. They were thinking Alejo had been in this country for twenty years, and yet what did he have? But no one said this. They just put hands on hands and gave many kisses and said, "I can't believe I'm seeing you here." They were all so skinny° and exhausted-looking, Luisa, Virginia, Maria, and Pedro. They came holding cloth bags with all their worldly possessions: a few crucifixes,° a change of clothing, aspirins given to them at the airport, an album of old photographs, prayer medals, a Bible, a few Cuban coins from the old days, and a throat-lozenge tin filled with some soil° from Holguín, Oriente province, Cuba.

2   After kissing and hugging them Alejo took them into the kitchen where they almost died.° There was so much of everything! Milk and wine and beer, steaks and rice and chicken and sausages and ham and plantains and ice cream and black bean soup and Pepsi-Cola and Hershey chocolate bars and almond nougat, and popcorn and Wise potato chips and Jiffy peanut butter, and rum and whiskey, marshmallows, spaghetti, flan and pasteles and chocolate cake and pie, more than enough to make them delirious.° And even though the walls were cracked and it was dark, there was a television set and a radio and

exhausted: very tired

in a trance: in a stunned, sleep-like condition

dreary: sad, depressing

skinny: very thin

crucifixes: Christian religious symbols (crosses)

soil: earth

almost died: were in a state of shock (idiomatic)

delirious: wild with emotion

lightbulbs and toilet paper and pictures of the family and crucifixes and
toothpaste and soap and more.

3   It was "Thank God for freedom and bless my family" from
Luisa's mouth, but her daughters were more cautious.° Distrusting the
world, they approached everything timidly. In the food-filled kitchen
Alejo told them how happy he was to have them in his house, and they
were happy because the old misery was over, but they were still without
a home and in a strange world. Uncertainty showed in their faces.

                                                                   cautious: careful

4   Pedro, Virginia's husband, managed to be the most cheerful. He
smoked and talked up a storm about the conditions in Cuba and the
few choices the Castro government had left to them. Smoking thick,
black cigars, Horacio and Alejo nodded and agreed, and the
conversation went back and forth and always ended with "What are
you going to do?"

5   "Work until I have something," was Pedro's simple answer. ◆

3. Focused Reading

*The visitors have ambivalent or conflicting feelings about the new
world they have come to. As you reread the text, take notes on what
the visitors feel positive about and what they feel negative about.*

+ Positive +	– Negative –
They're happy to see their relatives.	"dreary surroundings"

Share your notes with a partner. Then discuss this question: **Are
your feelings about life in North America ambivalent?**
Share one or two positive feelings and one or two negative ones.

4. Analyze the Story

In groups, choose one of the following to discuss. Elect a group member to report your conclusions to the class.

A. Based on this text, what can you conclude about the visitors' life in Cuba? What did they have? What didn't they have? Did they love their country?

B. Study paragraph 2. Why did the author name so many foods? What is the effect? Would you have written the paragraph differently?

C. If you have Cuban classmates, prepare questions you would like to ask about this text.

5. Look at Language

To read efficiently, you should not rely too heavily on a dictionary. Try to develop your guessing ability when you encounter new words. Sometimes the context of a new word will help you get the idea of the word.

Practice using the context to guess the meanings of the words and phrases in bold. Then tell the class what helped you guess each item.

1. "Seeing the arrival from the window, Mercedes was in a trance for a moment and then removed her **apron** and ran out, almost falling down the front steps. . . ." (paragraph 1)

   a. a button-down heavy sweater

   b. a cloth worn while cooking to protect one's clothing

   c. a large, decorative mirror

2. "The female cousins waited humbly, and then they began kissing Mercedes and Alejo and Hector and Horacio, their hats coming off and teeth chattering and hair getting all **snarled** like ivy on an old church. . . ." (paragraph 1)

   a. disordered and tangled

   b. dirty

   c. clean and shiny

3. "The female cousins, like china dolls, were incredibly beautiful, but were **struck dumb** by the snow and the new world, silent because there was something dreary about their surroundings." (paragraph 1)

   a. were completely covered

   b. were excited and happy

   c. were made speechless

4. "And even though the walls were **cracked** and it was dark, there was a television set and a radio and lightbulbs and toilet paper and pictures of the family and crucifixes and toothpaste and soap and more." (paragraph 2)

   a. decorated with pictures

   b. broken or split into two parts

   c. freshly painted

6. Move Beyond the Story

Discussion

A. The visitors brought their most precious possessions with them: crucifixes, photographs, a Bible, old Cuban coins, and soil from their region in Cuba.

   What important things did you carry here from your country? Think of three things, and tell why you needed to take them with you.

B. Upon arrival in New York, Luisa says, "Thank God for freedom." What does she mean? With a group, list reasons why refugees, immigrants, and students come to North America. Then discuss this question: Do most of these people find what they are looking for?

Writing

A. The author describes the female cousins in the following manner: "The female cousins, like china dolls, were incredibly beautiful." Write five sentences describing five people you know. Use the comparative word **like** as in the author's example.
Other Examples: My sister, like an oak tree, is tall and strong.
Ivan, like the sun, radiates warmth.

B. On a sheet of paper make two lists with these headings: "What I Like about Life in North America" and "What I Dislike about Life in North America." After you have written several ideas in each list, write an essay explaining your opinions and feelings about your life here. Give reasons if you can.

Challenge

Meet the Author

JAMAICA KINCAID *(born 1949)*

JAMAICA KINCAID was born and educated in Antigua, an island in the Caribbean. She is the author of several highly praised books and has become a prominent figure in American literature. The following excerpt is from her 1988 novel *Lucy*. Like all of Ms. Kincaid's work, *Lucy* has a poetic literary style, filled with imagery.

Ms. Kincaid lives with her husband and children in Bennington, Vermont.

1. Anticipate the Story

The following passage is the beginning of the novel *Lucy*. The novel tells the story of nineteen-year-old Lucy, who leaves her home in Antigua and comes to urban North America to care for some children and attend college. The book begins with her arrival.

Find Antigua on the map on page 180. Then read the title and first two sentences of the text. Try to predict Lucy's reaction when she first sees urban North America. What things might be different from Antigua? Write your ideas here.

_____

_____

_____

_____

_____

> **READING STRATEGY**
>
> Read a short, difficult text quickly the first time to get the overall picture.

2. Global Reading

Read the passage through as quickly as you can to get the general idea. Don't stop at new words. Were your predictions above correct?

Jot down your reactions or questions about the passage here or in your journal. Then share them with a partner or group.

reader response

....

....

....

....

....

....

....

....

....

....

....

Poor Visitor

◆◆◆

Jamaica Kincaid

IT WAS MY FIRST DAY. I had come the night before, a gray-black and cold night before—as it was expected to be in the middle of January, though I didn't know that at the time—and I could not see anything clearly on the way from the airport, even though there were lights everywhere. As we drove along, someone would single out° to me a famous building, an important street, a park, a bridge that when built was thought to be a spectacle.° In a daydream I used to have, all these places were points of happiness to me; all these places were lifeboats° to my small drowning° soul°, for I would imagine myself entering and leaving them, and just that—entering and leaving over and over again—would see me through° a bad feeling I did not have a name for. I only knew it felt a little like sadness but heavier than that. Now that I saw these places, they looked ordinary, dirty, worn down by so many people entering and leaving them in real life, and it occurred to me that I could not be the only person in the world for whom they were a fixture of fantasy. It was not my first bout° with the disappointment of reality and it would not be my last. The undergarments that I wore were all new, bought for my journey, and as I sat in the car, twisting° this way and that to get a good view of the sights before me, I was reminded of how uncomfortable the new can make you feel.

2   I got into an elevator, something I had never done before, and then I was in an apartment and seated at a table, eating food just taken from a refrigerator. In the place I had just come from, I always lived in a house, and my house did not have a refrigerator in it. Everything I was experiencing—the ride in the elevator, being in an apartment, eating day-old food that had been stored° in a refrigerator—was such a good idea that I could imagine I would grow used to it and like it very much, but at first it was all so new that I had to smile with my mouth turned down at the corners. I slept soundly that night, but it wasn't because I was happy and comfortable—quite the opposite; it was because I didn't want to take in° anything else.

3   That morning, the morning of my first day, the morning that followed my first night, was a sunny morning. It was not the sort of bright sun-yellow making everything curl° at the edges, almost in fright, that I

single out: point out, show

spectacle: something remarkable to look at

lifeboat: a boat to rescue people

drowning: sinking under water

soul: the spiritual part of a person

see me through: help me survive

bout: struggle, fight

twisting: turning

stored: kept

take in: absorb, receive, learn

curl: have a bent or curved shape

was used to, but a pale-yellow sun, as if the sun had grown weak from trying too hard to shine; but still it was sunny, and that was nice and made me miss my home less. And so, seeing the sun, I got up and put on a dress, a gay dress made out of madras° cloth—the same sort of dress that I would wear if I were at home and setting out for a day in the country. It was all wrong. The sun was shining but the air was cold. It was the middle of January, after all. But I did not know that the sun could shine and the air remain cold; no one had ever told me. What a feeling that was! How can I explain? Something I had always known—the way I knew my skin was the color brown of a nut rubbed repeatedly with a soft cloth, or the way I knew my own name—something I took completely for granted,° "the sun is shining, the air is warm," was not so. I was no longer in a tropical zone, and this realization now entered my life like a flow of water dividing formerly dry and solid ground, creating two banks,° one of which was my past—so familiar and predictable that even my unhappiness then made me happy now just to think of it—the other my future, a gray blank, an overcast seascape on which rain was falling and no boats were in sight. I was no longer in a tropical zone and I felt cold inside and out, the first time such a sensation had come over me. ◆

madras: a bright-colored, striped cloth

took for granted: considered as true

banks: two sides of a river or stream

3. Focused Reading

As you reread, complete this "map" showing things that were new or surprising to Lucy during her first few days in North America.

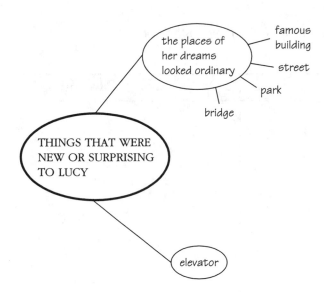

Did any of the same things surprise you? Tell a partner or the class.

4. Analyze the Story

In groups, choose one of the following to discuss. Elect a group member to report your conclusions to the class.

A. What kind of girl is Lucy? What can you guess about her from these pages? Underline parts of the text that support your ideas.

B. If you were making a film of these pages, what would the viewer see?

C. Do these first few pages of the novel *Lucy* make you want to read more? Why or why not?

5. Look at Language

A. A **motif** is an image or idea that is repeated throughout a text. In this text, the author uses a weather motif to compare Lucy's old and new homes.

Find weather-related words and phrases. Put them in the correct column.

Lucy's New Home	Lucy's Old Home
gray-black and cold night	

Why does the author use these weather details? What is the effect?

B. *Look at the words in bold. Which is an adjective and which is a noun?*

> (It was) a pale-yellow **sun**, as if the **sun** had grown weak from trying too hard to shine; but still it was **sunny**. . . .

Make adjectives from these weather-related nouns.

storm _stormy_ _____   smog _smoggy_ _____

snow _____   mist _____

fog _____   breeze _____

wind _____   rain _____

ice _____   steam _____

6. Move Beyond the Story

Discussion

Lucy was surprised by a number of things in North America. Take a survey of your classmates. Ask: What surprised you most about North America? After you collect your answers, make a chart showing the results. Try to group similar answers into categories if you can.

Writing

A. Lucy was disappointed when she arrived in North America because the reality did not match her dreams and fantasies. Did you have a similar experience with "the disappointment of reality"? Write about your first impressions of North America.

B. This text was the beginning of the novel *Lucy*. A bit later in the novel, the reader learns that Lucy is living with an American family and caring for their children while going to school. Rewrite the story of Lucy's arrival from the point of view of either parent.

UNIT 1 ◆ *Review*

◆◆◆◆◆◆◆◆◆◆◆◆◆◆◆◆◆◆◆◆◆◆◆◆◆◆◆◆◆◆◆◆

Texts	Main Characters
EXILE	Eva her parents
VISITORS, 1965	the visitors the Santinio family
POOR VISITOR	Lucy

Work individually, with a partner, or with a group to complete one
of these tasks.

1. Take a class survey. Ask: **Which text did you like best?
   Why?** Post your results on a bulletin board.

2. Compare how Lucy, the visiting cousins, and Eva see their
   futures. What are the similarities? What are the differences?

3. The following themes are repeated in at least two, and
   sometimes all three, of the texts. Discuss where the theme occurs
   and its importance in each text.

   A. SLEEP

   B. FOOD

   C. WEATHER

Learning English

© Ken Light

READING STRATEGY

Writing down what you
know or think about a
topic before reading
will help you get "into"
the topic.

The three writings in
this unit deal with
learning English. In
your journal, write
about *your*
experience learning
English. What
problems or
successes have you
had? What are you
afraid of? What
learning strategies
do you use? What
helps you most?

Meet the Author

PAT MORA

PAT MORA is a second-generation Mexican American. She grew up in El Paso, Texas, on the border of Mexico. She has written several volumes of poetry, as well as children's books and essays. She has received many creative writing awards. The following poem is from her 1984 volume of poetry, *Chants*.

Ms. Mora lives in Cincinnati, Ohio.

1. Anticipate the Poem

The poem on the next page is about Elena, a woman who thinks that learning English is very important for her future.

Before reading, write down why you are learning English. What are your goals? Tell a partner.

_____

_____

_____

_____

☞ READING STRATEGY

Good readers link what they read with their own experience.

2. Global Reading

Read the poem through without stopping. Is Elena studying English for the same reasons you are?

Do you share any of Elena's problems or feelings? Jot down any other reactions or questions you have about the poem here or in your journal. Share them with a partner or group.

☞ HOW YOU READ

Did you enjoy reading this? Why or why not?

reader response

Elena

◆◆

Pat Mora

My Spanish isn't enough.
I remember how I'd smile
listening to my little ones,
understanding every word they'd say,
their jokes, their songs, their plots.°
5   *Vamos a pedirle dulces a mamá. Vamos.**
But that was in Mexico.
Now my children go to American high schools.
They speak English. At night they sit around
the kitchen table, laugh with one another.
10 I stand by the stove and feel dumb,° alone.
I bought a book to learn English.
My husband frowned,° drank more beer.
My oldest said, "*Mamá*, he doesn't want you
to be smarter than he is." I'm forty,
15 embarrassed at mispronouncing words,
embarrassed at the laughter of my children,
the grocer, the mailman. Sometimes I take
my English book and lock myself in the bathroom,
say the thick words softly,
20 for if I stop trying, I will be deaf °
when my children need my help. ◆

plots: secret projects, conspiracies

dumb: 1) unable to speak, 2) stupid

frowned: made a disapproving face

deaf: unable to hear

---

*Spanish for "Let's go ask mom for candy. Come on."

3. Focused Reading

As you reread, think about the relationship among (a) Elena, (b) her husband, (c) their children, and (d) the local community. How has it changed since Mexico? Will it be different in the future? Complete the figure below. Draw the characters where they belong in relation to each other and to the community.

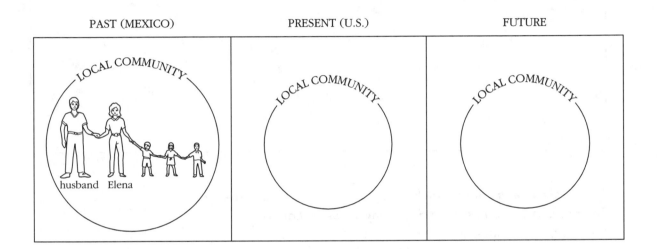

PAST (MEXICO)   PRESENT (U.S.)   FUTURE

Compare your drawings with a partner's. How are they similar? How are they different?

4. Analyze the Poem

In groups, choose one of the following to discuss. Elect a group member to report your conclusions to the class.

A. What obstacles stand in the way of Elena's learning English? List them. Do you think she will be successful in overcoming these obstacles?

B. What is Elena's approach to studying English? How does she practice? Do you have any advice for her?

C. How does Elena feel about her situation? Choose from the following list, and support your ideas: *optimistic, pessimistic, amused, fearful, frustrated, angry, confused, determined, happy,* _____ (other).

5. Look at Language

Which words or phrases in the poem evoke an emotion? Classify them as positive or negative emotions.

+ Positive +	– Negative –
smile	

*Elena **mispronounces** words; she pronounces them incorrectly. The prefix **mis-** can be added to many verbs. What do the following verbs mean?*

misspeak	misinform	misquote
misuse	misread	mishear
misunderstand	misspell	misplace
mislead	misjudge	mistrust

Fill in the blanks with one of the words above. Use the correct tense.

1. Yesterday's newspaper _____ the president's comments.

2. I _____ my glasses; I can't find them anywhere.

3. If you check a dictionary, you won't _____ words in your essays.

4. I _____ the map and got totally lost.

5. "I'm sorry I _____ you about the meeting. It's Tuesday at 3:00 P.M., not Wednesday."

6. Move Beyond the Poem

Discussion

A. What can you infer (guess) about Elena's husband and her relationship with him? How does he compare with men you know?

B. Pronouncing English words seems especially difficult for Elena. What is most difficult for you in learning English? Why? Ask classmates for advice.

Writing

A. Can you identify with Elena's embarrassment? Tell about a time when you felt embarrassed because of a language problem.

B. How are you similar to or different from Elena? Use a Venn diagram to jot down your ideas before writing.

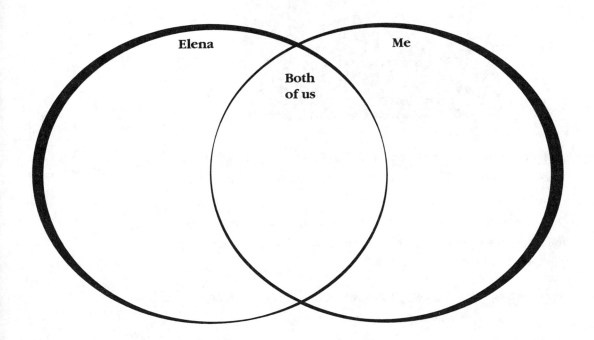

C. Write a letter to the poet telling your impressions of the poem. Send it to her c/o Arte Público Press, University of Houston, Houston, TX 77204-2090.

Meet the Author

ANDREI CODRESCU *(born 1946)*

ANDREI CODRESCU was born in Romania. In 1966, at the age of twenty, he came to the United States. Mr. Codrescu has written more than twenty books in English, his second language. He is a poet, essayist, novelist, radio commentator, and film director. The following essay is taken from his 1986 essay collection, *A Craving for Swan.*

Mr. Codrescu lives in New Orleans, Louisiana, and teaches English at Louisiana State University in Baton Rouge.

1. Anticipate the Essay

In this humorous essay, the author, who speaks many languages, discusses his language learning experiences. He contrasts learning in school (in Romania) with learning outside of school.

Find Romania on the map on page 181.

Write a sentence or two about your own learning of English in and out of school. Where do you learn better? Why? Tell a partner.

_____

_____

_____

_____

_____

> **READING STRATEGY**
>
> Read a difficult text the first time for the general idea. Use the context to get the meaning of some new words. Remember you don't need to know every word to get the general idea.

2. Global Reading

Read the essay through to get the general idea. Compare your learning experiences with the writer's. Are yours similar or different?

Jot down your reactions or questions about the essay here or in your journal. Share them with a partner or group.

> **HOW YOU READ**
>
> Which new words could you understand from the context?

> **reader response**

Languages

◆◆

Andrei Codrescu

WHEN PEOPLE ASK ME HOW MANY LANGUAGES I SPEAK and I tell them, they are always amazed. "It's a sad thing," they say, "but Americans rarely speak another language." Some of them blame the educational system, while others bemoan the insularity ° of the natives, while others yet attribute the deficiency ° to arrogance.°

2   All of these are in some measure true. The teaching of languages in school is a disaster. But my own linguistic education did not take place in school. On second thought, wait! I did learn one word: *okno*, which is Russian for window. I was in love with my Russian teacher, Comrade Papadopolou, who wore the first miniskirt in Romania, possibly in Eastern Europe. I stared at her in a daze for four years. Once she looked directly at me, and I looked out the window, which caused her to say *okno*.

3   It was worse with French, which was taught by a very strict pedagogue° of the old school who corrected the misconjugation of verbs with a rap° across the knuckles. In her presence I automatically conjugated anything that came to mind, and later, when I went to France, I could not keep myself from conjugating when the present tense would have sufficed.° Once, in a café, I said to the waiter: "J'ai faim!" (I am hungry), and before I could check myself I said: "Tu as faim, il a faim, nous avons faim, vous avez faim, ils ont faim!"*

4   But if French was bad, nothing was as hideous as Latin. Even the Romans, I am sure, had been bored stiff by the rhetors° we were forced to translate two thousand years later.

5   So convinced was I that I was terrible in languages, that when I left Romania I considered pretending to be a deaf-mute° in order to get by.°

6   But then a miracle° happened. As soon as I came into the presence of real people, understanding came to me. The small tasks of daily life—getting about, eating, and buying necessities—were the best teachers.

insularity: isolation

deficiency: lack, inadequacy

arrogance: self-importance

pedagogue: a narrow-minded teacher

rap: a sharp hit

would have sufficed: would have been enough

rhetors: people who give speeches

deaf-mute: a person unable to hear and speak

get by: survive (colloquial)

miracle: a supernatural event

---

*French for "You are hungry, he is hungry, we are hungry, you are hungry, they are hungry!"

7   The first sentence of English I ever put together was: "Why don't you kill yourself?" Actually, my Romanian friend Julian put it together and he was very proud of it. We spent the day testing it on the unsuspecting. "Why don't you kill yourself?" I asked a group of loiterers° by the train station in Rome. After much deliberation° among themselves they directed us to the self-service machines at the station, which is what they thought we wanted to know. Ever since, I think of "self" as a coin-operated vending machine.

8   When I came to America, I had no end of trouble.° People here just don't understand how there could be anything but English in the world. I was thrown off buses, scowled at in greasy spoons,° and ordered out of 7-Elevens.° But eventually I absorbed English just as I absorbed all the others: by osmosis.° The language seeped in, making itself a home in me as I was making myself a home in it.

9   A foreign language isn't just words. It is another view of the world. "House" and "maison"* are not the same thing, though they might translate similarly. Because of this, it is nearly impossible to learn a language without knowing the place and the people who speak it. Words come with gestures, gestures come with landscapes. Words are alive, inhabited.

10   This isn't to say that I approve of the disastrous state of foreign language instruction in America. Provincialism° begins precisely with neglect.° ◆

loiterers: people standing around doing nothing

deliberation: discussion

no end of trouble: constant trouble

greasy spoons: cheap restaurants (slang)

7-Eleven: the name of a minimarket

osmosis: in biology, when a liquid goes through the wall of a cell

provincialism: looking at life with a limited view

neglect: lack of care

---

*French for "house."

3. Focused Reading

Reread the essay. Try to summarize in one or two sentences the author's experiences in and out of school.

His experiences learning in school	His experiences learning out of school

Share your summaries with a partner or group. Then talk about these questions: How did you learn languages in your country? Are methods there similar to methods described in the essay? To methods in North America?

4. Analyze the Essay

In groups, choose one of the following to discuss. Elect a group member to report your conclusions to the class.

A. Talk about how the essay is organized. Paragraph 1 is the introduction. What is the main idea of paragraphs 2–5? Could these paragraphs appear in a different order or would the essay lose something?

What is the function of paragraph 6? What is the main idea of paragraphs 6–9?

B. The tone of this essay is humorous. We laugh because the writer *exaggerates*—he overstates and stretches the truth. With your group, underline the places in the essay where you see *exaggeration*.

C. What does the author say about America and the Americans? Do you agree or disagree? Support your opinion with examples.

5. Look at Language

To read efficiently, you should not rely too heavily on a dictionary. Try to develop your guessing ability when you encounter new words. Sometimes the **context** of a new word, that is, the words or sentences that come before or after a new word, will help you get the idea of the word.

Practice using the context to guess the meanings of the words and phrases in bold. Then tell the class what helped you guess each item.

1. "I was in love with my Russian teacher, Comrade Papadopolou, who wore the first miniskirt in Romania, possibly in Eastern Europe. I stared at her **in a daze** for four years." (paragraph 2)

    a. coldly

    b. in a state of boredom

    c. in a dreamy, silly way

2. "It was worse with French, which was taught by a very **strict** pedagogue of the old school who corrected the misconjugation of verbs with a rap across the knuckles." (paragraph 3)

    a. rigid and inflexible

    b. gentle and sweet

    c. intelligent

3. "But if French was bad, nothing was as **hideous** as Latin. Even the Romans, I am sure, had been bored stiff by the rhetors we were forced to translate two thousand years later." (paragraph 4)

   a. awful

   b. interesting

   c. difficult

4. "When I came to America, I had no end of trouble. People here just don't understand how there could be anything but English in the world. I was thrown off buses, **scowled at** in greasy spoons, and ordered out of 7-Elevens." (paragraph 8)

   a. helped

   b. given angry looks

   c. smiled at

6. Move Beyond the Essay

Discussion

A. The author writes, "When I came to America, I had no end of trouble. People here just don't understand how there could be anything but English in the world. I was thrown off buses, scowled at in greasy spoons, and ordered out of 7-Elevens." Are the author's opinions and experiences similar to your own? (Keep in mind that he may be exaggerating somewhat for comic effect.)

B. The author writes, "The small tasks of daily life—getting about, eating, and buying necessities—were the best teachers [of English]." Outside of school, what (or who) helps you learn English? Fill out the following questionnaire. Share your responses with a group.

Language-Learning Questionnaire

— I listen to music in English.
— I listen to books on tape.
— I listen to tapes that I make of conversations.
— I listen to the radio.
— I watch TV. (which programs?) _____
— I watch movies.

— I talk to my neighbors.
— I talk to myself in English.
— I try to talk to strangers. (where?) _____
— I talk to English-speaking friends.
— I have a regular conversation partner.

— I read a daily newspaper. (which one?} _____
— I read signs on the street.
— I read magazines.
— I read other things. (what?) _____

— I write a daily journal.
— I write letters in English.
— I write other things. (what?) _____

— (other) _____
— (other) _____

Writing

A. Write about the language classes you have taken here or in your country. Are your experiences similar to the author's?

B. Write about what works best for you in your study of English. Use your responses to the questionnaire as a starting point.

Challenge

Meet the Author

KIM YONG IK *(born 1920)*

KIM YONG IK was born in South Korea and educated in Seoul and Tokyo. At the age of twenty-eight, he came to the United States to study English literature at Florida Southern College, the University of Kentucky, and the University of Iowa. His short stories have been published in major North American magazines, and his novels have won numerous awards. The following autobiographical story first appeared in *The Writer* in 1965. Mr. Kim has taught at Korea University in Seoul as well as at various American universities.

Mr. Kim Yong Ik lives with his wife in Pittsburgh, Pennsylvania.

1. Anticipate the Story

In the following autobiographical story, the Korean-born author writes about how he pursued his dream in North America.

Find South Korea on the map on page 181.
Read the first paragraph. What kind of person is the author? With the class, write two or three questions you would like answered as you read.

Question: _____

_____

Question: _____

_____

Question: _____

_____

> **READING STRATEGY**
>
> Asking yourself questions before and while you read can help you focus and comprehend.

2. Global Reading

Read the story as quickly as you can to get the main ideas and to find answers to your questions.

Jot down your reactions or questions about the story here or in your journal. Share them with a partner or group.

reader response

A Book-Writing Venture

Kim Yong Ik

IN 1948 WHEN I STARTED TO WRITE A NOVEL apart from my regular school work at Florida Southern College, Lakeland, Florida, my roommate in the dormitory told me, "If I were you, I wouldn't waste time in this country. I'll give you five hundred dollars if you publish one book in America. Breaking into that racket° is nearly impossible even for an American writer who has mastered his own language." I was far from a master of English, but I didn't listen to him inside. I had studied English literature during the Second World War when it was a most unpopular subject to take up in the Orient, but I wanted to study it. Once in America, I wanted to write so much that I refused to accept the fact that my English was far from being adequate to write a novel. I put in° three hours early every morning writing a book.

2   The language problem that I was attacking loomed° larger and larger as I began to learn more. When I would describe in English certain concepts and objects enmeshed in° Korean emotion and imagination, I became slowly aware of nuances,° of differences between two languages even in simple expression. The remark "Kim entered the house" seems to be simple enough, yet unless a reader has a clear visual image of a Korean house, his understanding of the sentence is not complete. When a Korean says he is "in the house," he may be in his courtyard, or on his porch,° or in his small room! If I wanted to give a specific picture of entering the house in the Western sense, I had to say "room" instead of house—sometimes. I say, "sometimes" because many Koreans entertain their guests on their porches and still are considered to be hospitable,° and in the Korean sense, going into the "room" may be a more intimate act than it would be in the English sense. Such problems! That is merely an example. My Florida friends tried to help.

3   After three years in Florida, I moved to the University of Kentucky to continue my book-writing venture. During a holiday season when I was hired by the library to wax° some leather-bound° books, for fifty cents an hour, I often daydreamed that some day I

breaking into that racket: getting started in this business (colloquial)

put in: worked

loomed: slowly appeared

enmeshed in: interconnected with

nuances: small differences

porch: an open room attached to a house

hospitable: friendly, welcoming

wax: treat with a substance made from beeswax or paraffin

leather-bound: covered with animal skin

would have my book published and bound in that shining, aromatic° leather. I was all by myself in the Precious Books section upstairs. While working with the bindings° with my hands full of grease and wax, I would read aloud from a book of poetry open before me. Reading poetry did not require me to turn pages often. I also loved the rhythmical voice in it. Each time my reading was interrupted because with dirty hands I could not turn the page immediately, I was frustrated, as though a phonograph record got stuck in a scratch° on a recording of my favorite song. As I was reading Robert Frost's* "The Road Not Taken," I saw the librarian in charge of the section standing right behind me. I knew that she would chide° me or even dismiss° me, for the library was strict about student workers reading during their work hours. I couldn't look up at her to say hello. I saw her dry hand reach for the book, as though she would take it away; instead, her fingers turned the page for me to go on, and she left the room without saying a word! I was deeply moved° as I finished the poem—"And that has made all the difference."

4   I did go on to finish writing my book. In 1953 when I enrolled in the Writers Workshop of the University of Iowa, I had been writing fiction for six years and had completed one novel. I started to send it to various publishers in New York.

5   I had to send it by railway express and had to pay return postage. This amounted to nearly five dollars for each mailing. Since it took about a month for the rejected° manuscript° to reach me, this turned out to be a regular monthly expense. I would walk to the outskirts of Iowa City to the railroad station to save the bus fare that would help pay for mailing the manuscript. The railway express man was quite curious about the mysterious package that kept reappearing, and finally he asked me what was in it.

6   I explained to him, and he told me there was an old man in Iowa City who kept on mailing his manuscript about every month, just as I did.

7   Still I appeared so often that finally I was embarrassed whenever I met the express agent. We got to know each other rather well. By this time, he knew that Korean was my mother tongue;

---

*A famous American poet (1874–1963).

aromatic: sweet-smelling

bindings: the covers of a book

scratch: a rough spot

chide: find fault angrily

dismiss: fire; let go from a job

moved: emotionally affected

rejected: refused

manuscript: an unpublished work

Japanese my second (I had learned this under the Japanese occupation); and English my third (I started to learn English during my high school days in Korea). One day I asked him what had become of the old man and his manuscript, and he said, "That fellow's manuscript always came back but he is now dead."

8   I kept up° the game of mailing and receiving my novel manuscript, as well as several short stories. I felt I was making some progress in mastering the English language even if my collection of rejection slips° seemed to shout otherwise. As days and seasons passed, I became more desperate. I read and wrote harder than before. Even on the train on the way to Maine to work for a family for the summer, I kept up my morning ritual of three hours of writing. By day, I read stories for their children, enjoying the rhythm of the English language. At night, I stayed up late writing. Word got around° that the Korean "liked to sleep with his light on."

9   I returned to school that fall only to write. My landlady in Iowa City would complain that I did not leave the room on the weekend so she could properly clean my room, and further remarked that she wouldn't like her boy to go abroad just to stay in a room always. I listened to her advice only to learn living language.

10   I would walk around with a night watchman or with janitors on night duty, and from them I would have free lessons of English—by listening. When I went to work at the University Hospital cafeteria across the Iowa River, I used to copy a poem or two on a slip of paper to read on the way. In the cafeteria I kept the slip of paper hidden under the counter and tried to memorize it while serving food. Of course, I was fired after two weeks.

11   I actually cared very little about a degree, so there was very small satisfaction in academic success. I wanted to have one story accepted. I was beginning to feel that perhaps this would never happen. I had only my many rejection slips to contemplate°—after so many years of labor.°

12   One Saturday it was snowing really hard outside. I was filled with self-doubt and wondered how in the world I had acquired the fantastic idea that I could write the drama of human emotion in fiction in a second language—no, in my third. I was feeling so dejected° that I went out and spent nearly all my money on a record player. At least I

kept up: continued

rejection slips: notices from publishers that work is not accepted

word got around: the news spread (colloquial)

contemplate: look at; think about

labor: hard work

dejected: very sad

could have music. Then I borrowed a record of Antonio Vivaldi's* *Four Seasons* from the library and played it over and over that day, not even stopping to eat.

13   As I sat listening and watching the falling snow, I had a strange fantasy. I imagined that I saw a pair of Korean wedding shoes walking away from me in the show. I followed the shoes in my mind, but I was always behind the figure who wore them, watching the back of the silk brocade shoes and the white muslin socks. The silken wedding shoes walked on and on toward the distant hills. I wanted to discover the person who wore the shoes, but she and her shoes wouldn't turn so I could see her. I heard my heart beat as I ran after the footmarks not to lose sight of the beautiful shoes, fearing that the snow might be wetting the finest silk.

14   I thought that if only I could see the elusive° owner of these shoes, then I could write a real story! I came out of my reverie° and got up determined to do just that. . . .

elusive: hard to catch
reverie: daydream; fantasy

15   When I completed "The Wedding Shoes," I gave it to Paul Eagle, the director of the Writers Workshop, but he was busy at the time and gave it to Margarette Young, author of *The Angel of the Forest.* She called me up and said with great enthusiasm, "This is wonderful. You must send this story to *Harper's Bazaar* right away." I did.

16   A few weeks later I found a letter in my mail box instead of the familiar ugly yellowed package. Alice Morris, the literary editor of *Harper's Bazaar*, wrote me that she wanted to print my story and would pay me $250. It was a time of great joy, but I had no one to share it with.

17   Soon after my story appeared, *London Bazaar* cabled me: "Offer twenty-five guineas for 'The Wedding Shoes.'" About the same time, an amateur ballet group in Iowa City planned a ballet based on my story—so, on an electric light pole in front of the grocery store was posted an advertising poster: "A Ballet: The Silken Brocade Shoes."

18   After my stories had been accepted by *Mademoiselle, Botteghe Oscure,* and *The New Yorker*, I returned to my homeland after spending ten years in America. Besides my teaching at a university, I continued

---

*An Italian composer from the eighteenth century.

to write in English as well as in my native tongue. In 1960 I revisited the United States to see my old friends. I was happy to find the librarian at the Precious Books section when I dropped in° at the University of Kentucky. She remembered my reading poetry during my work hours and even the incident of turning the page for me. She asked me what I had been doing. When I mentioned what I had written for magazines, that I'd had juvenile° books published by Little, Brown, and that an adult novel of mine was to be published by Alfred A. Knopf, she did not believe me until she looked them up in the publication index of the library. Then she was so happy for me that she invited me for dinner in a Chinese restaurant, and later we drove around in that bluegrass country.

dropped in: visited (colloquial)

juvenile: children's

19   That winter, I received a Christmas gift from Little, Brown—a copy of my first juvenile fiction book, written in Florida and Kentucky— *The Happy Days*, bound in beautiful leather. ♦

3. Focused Reading

The events in this story are written in sequence, or chronological order. As you reread, take notes on how the author moves toward his two goals of mastering English and becoming a published writer.

Date	Place	What are his strategies for mastering English?	Does he move toward his goal of being a published writer?
1948	Florida Southern College	He writes *a lot*. He gets help from friends.	Yes, he starts writing a novel. (He sees many problems, though.)
1951	University of Kentucky		
Fall 1953	University of Iowa		
Summer 1954	Maine		
Fall 1954	University of Iowa		
1958	Korea		

Which of the author's strategies have you tried or would you like to try?

4. Analyze the Story

In groups, choose one of the following to discuss. Elect a group member to report your conclusions to the class.

A. If you were the author of this story, what title would you have given it? List other possible titles.

B. What kind of a person is the author? List five adjectives. Support each idea with examples from the story. Is the author like you? How?

C. The author succeeded in reaching his goal. Who and what helped him? Make a list. Then answer this question: Who and what help you in moving toward your goals in this country?

5. Look at Language

There are many ways to indicate the time relationship between two events. Study the examples below.

Same Time

During his years in the United States, the author wrote a lot.

While he studied at the University of Kentucky, he worked in the library.

While studying at the University of Kentucky, he worked in the library.

As he worked in the library, he often read poetry.

When he heard that a story would be published, he was joyful.

When hearing that a story would be published, he was joyful.

NOTE: *while* = during the time (single or repeated occurrence)
     as = during the time (single occurrence)
     when = at the time

     during + noun
     while, as, when + clause

Continuation

After ten years in the United States, the author returned home.

After he had studied for ten years, the author returned home.

The author studied for ten years. **Then**, he returned home.

He left Korea in 1948. Ten years **later**, he returned home.

NOTE: *After* can connect two sentences; *then* and *later* do not.
     Be careful not to use *after* where you should use *then*.

Now look back at paragraphs 2–4 and 15–18 of the story. Circle an example of each of the above words. Study the way the author uses them.

6. Move Beyond the Story

Discussion

The author seems to find support and inspiration from poetry and classical music. Take a survey of your classmates. Find out what they like to do, read, listen to, or look at when they need inspiration or emotional support.

Writing

A. The author had a very clear goal in North America: "I wanted to have one story accepted." What are your goals in this country? Have they changed since you arrived? Tell how you are trying to achieve them.

B. The author clearly seems to love writing. Why do you think he likes it so much? Discuss how you feel about writing in English and in your native language.

UNIT 2 ◆ *Review*

◆◆◆◆◆◆◆◆◆◆◆◆◆◆◆◆◆◆◆◆◆◆◆◆◆◆◆◆◆◆◆◆◆◆◆◆◆

Texts	Main Characters
ELENA	Elena
LANGUAGES	the author, Andrei Codrescu
A BOOK-WRITING VENTURE	the author, Kim Yong Ik

Work individually, with a partner, or with a group to complete one of these tasks.

1. Take a class survey. Ask: **Which text did you like best? Why?** Post your results on a bulletin board.

2. Which character is

    a. the most interesting? _____

    b. the most likeable? _____

    c. the most serious? _____

    d. the most lighthearted? _____

    e. the most timid? _____

    f. the least timid? _____

    g. the best language learner? _____

    h. the most like you? _____

    Support your opinions.

3. Contrast the different English-learning strategies of the three characters. Whose approach to learning is the most like yours?

Feeling Homesick

The three stories in this unit are about homesickness. Write about homesickness in your journal. You can complete one or more of these ideas. I feel homesick when . . . . The things I miss most about home are . . . . I try to fight my homesickness by . . . .

Meet the Author

SANDRA CISNEROS *(born 1954)*

SANDRA CISNEROS was born in Chicago to a Mexican father and Mexican-American mother. An award-winning poet and fiction writer, she has emerged as a major figure in North American literature. Her work has been translated into seven languages. The following story comes from her prizewinning collection of stories, *The House on Mango Street* (1984).

Ms. Cisneros lives in San Antonio, Texas, where she is working on a new novel.

1. Anticipate the Story

The narrator of the following story is a young Mexican-American girl growing up in Chicago. She tells the story of Mamacita, a woman who has just moved to her neighborhood from Mexico.

Read the title, the first two paragraphs, and the first sentence of the third paragraph. With the class, write some questions you would like answered as you read.

Question: _____

_____

Question: _____

_____

Question: _____

_____

2. Global Reading

Read the story as quickly as you can. Did you find answers to any of your questions?

Jot down your reactions or questions about the story here or in your journal. Share them with a partner or group.

reader response

No Speak English

◆•◆

Sandra Cisneros

MAMACITA* IS THE BIG MAMA° of the man across the street, third-floor front. Rachel says her name ought to be *Mamasota,*† but I think that's mean.

big mama: wife (slang)

2   The man saved his money to bring her here. He saved and saved because she was alone with the baby boy in that country. He worked two jobs. He came home late and he left early. Every day.

3   Then one day Mamacita and the baby boy arrived in a yellow taxi. The taxi door opened like a waiter's arm. Out stepped a tiny pink shoe, a foot soft as a rabbit's ear, then the thick ankle, a flutter° of hips, fuchsia° roses and green perfume. The man had to pull her, the taxicab driver had to push. Push, pull. Push, pull. Poof!

flutter: a quick movement or vibration

fuchsia: purplish-red

4   All at once she bloomed.° Huge, enormous, beautiful to look at, from the salmon-pink feather on the tip of her hat down to the little rosebuds of her toes. I couldn't take my eyes off her tiny shoes.

bloomed: flowered

5   Up, up, up the stairs she went with the baby boy in a blue blanket, the man carrying her suitcases, her lavender° hatboxes, a dozen boxes of satin high heels.° Then we didn't see her.

lavender: pale purple

high heels: shoes with tall heels

6   Somebody said because she's too fat, somebody because of the three flights of stairs, but I believe she doesn't come out because she is afraid to speak English, and maybe this is so since she only knows eight words. She knows to say: *He not here* for when the landlord comes, *No speak English* if anybody else comes, and *Holy smokes.* I don't know where she learned this, but I heard her say it one time and it surprised me.

7   My father says when he came to this country he ate hamandeggs for three months. Breakfast, lunch and dinner. Hamandeggs. That was the only word he knew. He doesn't eat hamandeggs anymore.

8   Whatever her reasons, whether she is fat, or can't climb the stairs, or is afraid of English, she won't come down. She sits all day by

---

*Spanish for "little woman."

†Spanish for "big woman."

the window and plays the Spanish radio show and sings all the homesick songs about her country in a voice that sounds like a seagull.

9   Home. Home. Home is a house in a photograph, a pink house, pink as hollyhocks° with lots of startled° light. The man paints the walls of the apartment pink, but it's not the same you know. She still sighs° for her pink house, and then I think she cries. I would.

10   Sometimes the man gets disgusted. He starts screaming and you can hear it all the way down the street.

11   Ay, she says, she is sad.

12   Oh, he says, not again.

13   ¿Cuándo, cuándo, cuándo?* she asks.

14   ¡Ay, Caray!† We *are* home. This *is* home. Here I am and here I stay. Speak English. Speak English! . . .

15   ¡Ay! Mamacita, who does not belong, every once in a while lets out a cry, hysterical, high, as if he had torn the only skinny thread that kept her alive, the only road out to that country.

16   And then to break her heart forever, the baby boy who has begun to talk, starts to sing the Pepsi commercial he heard on T.V.

17   No speak English, she says to the child who is singing in the language that sounds like tin.° No speak English, no speak English, and bubbles into tears. No, no, no as if she can't believe her ears. ◆

hollyhocks: plants with big, colorful flowers

startled: (here) bright, shocking

sighs: breathes slowly and sadly

tin: a soft metal

---

*Spanish for "When, when, when!"
†Spanish for "Oh brother."

3. Focused Reading

As you reread, think about Mamacita's life now and before. Fill in the chart with facts from the story and with your own conclusions.

Now (In the USA)	Before (In Her Country)
She lives in a city apartment.	She lived in a pink house (in the country?).

READING STRATEGY

When a text compares two things, you can make a chart like this to help you read, understand, and remember.

Discuss your chart with a partner. Then talk about your lives now and before. Are there any parallels with Mamacita's life?

If you have Mexican classmates, ask them any questions the story may have raised about Mexico.

4. Analyze the Story

In groups, choose one of the following to discuss. Elect a group member to report your conclusions to the class.

A. Why does Mamacita's heart break when her child sings the Pepsi commercial?

B. The young narrator says, "She still sighs for her pink house, and then I think she cries. I would." What does this indicate about the narrator?

C. The title of the story is "No Speak English." When Mamacita says these words to people who come to the apartment, what does she mean? _____
When she says the words to her son, what does she mean? _____

5. Look at Language

A. *What words and phrases in the story bring Mamacita alive? Circle the language that speaks to the senses: sight, touch, hearing, or smell. Categorize the words and phrases below.*

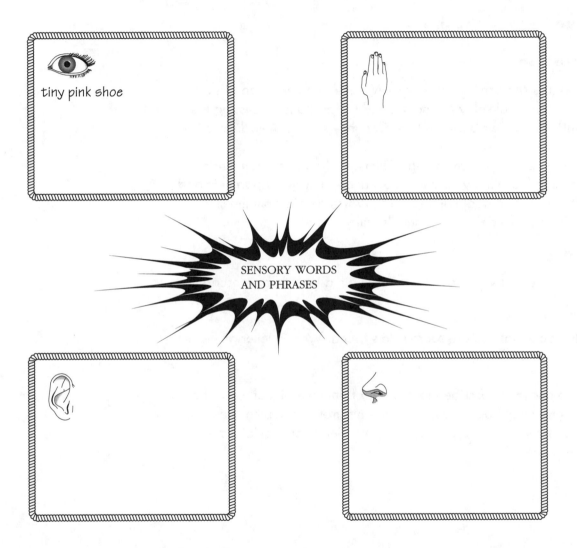

tiny pink shoe

SENSORY WORDS AND PHRASES

Share your categories with a partner or the class. What does all of this language reveal about Mamacita?

B. *The writer often repeats words and phrases in the story. Find examples of repetition like the following, and write them down. Why does the writer use this device?*

The man saved his money. . . . He saved and saved. . . .

6. Move Beyond the Story

Discussion

A. Discuss Mamacita's marriage. Will she and her husband stay together? Role-play Mamacita and her husband discussing their future and their baby's future. Can they resolve their dispute?

B. Imagine that you are going to film this short story. You must decide first what your characters and setting (the apartment and the neighborhood) will look like. Which details from the story will you include? Which details will you add?

Writing

A. Imagine that you are Mamacita. Write a letter home describing your new life.

B. Imagine that you are Mamacita's friend. Write a letter giving her some advice.

C. Mamacita is described in this story from the point of view of a young neighbor girl who watches her from across the street. Do you have an interesting neighbor or friend you would like to describe?

Meet the Author

LIU ZONGREN *(born 1940)*

LIU ZONGREN was born and raised in Beijing, China. He was the son of a peasant farmer who later became a self-made engineer. Liu Zongren is also a self-made man who taught himself English despite many difficulties. Although he did not start studying English until he was in his mid-twenties, Mr. Liu has written two books in English. The following text is taken from his best-selling autobiography, *Two Years in the Melting Pot* (1984), in which he tells about his experiences studying in the United States.

Mr. Liu lives with his wife and son in Beijing, where he works as a writer, journalist, and translator.

1. Anticipate the Story

In the following pages from *Two Years in the Melting Pot*, the author tells how he tries to fight loneliness while attending a university in Chicago. He describes some of his strategies for making new friends.

Have you made new friends here? How did you do it? Is it easy or difficult to meet people? Why? Write a sentence below summarizing your experience. Tell your classmates.

_____

_____

_____

_____

_____

> **READING STRATEGIES**
>
> 1. Good readers focus on major ideas the first time they read a difficult text.
> 2. They relate their own experience to what the author says.

2. Global Reading

Read the passage through as quickly as you can. Read to see if the author's experiences are similar to your own.

Jot down your reactions or questions about the passage here or in your journal. Then share them with a partner or group.

> **HOW YOU READ**
>
> Were you able to read quickly and focus on major ideas?

> **reader response**
>
> ....
>
> ....
>
> ....
>
> ....
>
> ....
>
> ....
>
> ....
>
> ....
>
> ....
>
> ....
>
> ....

Two Years in the Melting Pot

◆◆

Liu Zongren

I HAD TO FIND MORE FRIENDS. After several weeks in school I knew only a couple other students, and saw them only to talk to for a few minutes, perhaps three times a week. I decided I would get to know a few more names, at least, from my three classes. One day I came ten minutes early to my 11:00 A.M. News Media and U.S. Government class. Two young women, one black and one white, were already there. I told myself to be aggressive,° as Victor advised me to be, and went up to them.

aggressive: bold, active

2   "Hi." I tried to be casual.° "My name is Liu Zongren. I come from Beijing, China." I put stress on Beijing, hoping that might create some attention.

casual: informal

3   "Oh, really?" The white woman seemed interested. "How long have you been here?"

4   "Two months."

5   "How do you find it here?"

6   I couldn't understand what she meant. "I came here by plane, of course." I must have looked lost. The white woman added quickly, "I mean, do you like this country?"

7   "Well, I don't know." How foolish I was. Why had I said this?

8   "My name is Ann. This is Geri."

9   Geri was the black woman. She smiled at me. "I've learned Chinese."

10   "How nice," I smiled back. "How much do you know?" I was hoping this would make the conversation last longer than just a courteous° exchange.

courteous: polite

11   "I studied it only a few months and found it too difficult, so I dropped it."

12   "Yes, Chinese is a difficult language," I faltered, not knowing how to continue. You can carry on° a little more, I told myself. "Do you like this class?"

carry on: continue

13   The women nodded, "Yes." I cursed myself: why do you ask such a silly question? If they don't like it, why are they taking it? How stupid I am.

14   Several other students had come in by now and I didn't know if the two women wanted to go on talking. I began feeling nervous when I realized that I was standing in the middle of the classroom.

15   Ann started to move away. "Glad to meet you, Mr. —"

16   "Liu," I said hastily, "Just call me Liu. My last, no, my first name is too hard to pronounce."

17   "Glad to meet you, Mr. Liu," Ann repeated.

18   "Thank you," I said to them, my face flushed.° I wondered what I had thanked them for, as I made my way to a nearby seat.

flushed: red in the face

19   After the class began, most of what the professor said escaped my ears and I left as soon as the lecture was over. I had no other class that day and I didn't want to go back to the loneliness of the McKnight house, so I wandered around the campus. Many students were entering a particular lecture hall. I stopped and checked my timetable. It was a history class. Good.

20   I went in. It was a large classroom with at least eighty students already there, and more coming in. I selected a seat not too close to the lectern. Nobody paid any attention to me and I saw several oriental faces among the crowd. I relaxed, took out my notebook, and opened the campus newspaper, pretending to be an old hand.° A young man sat down beside me and smiled. My watch said it was five minutes until class. Perhaps I could strike up° a conversation with this young, friendly-looking man. I started my routine. "My name is Liu Zongren. I come from Beijing, China."

old hand: person with much experience

strike up: start

21   "Glad to meet you. My name is George Christi." He seemed in the mood to talk.

22   "Please write down your name for me." I handed my notebook over to him. "You know, it is very hard for me to remember American names without seeing them spelled out." I said this out of a desire to speak two more sentences, rather than as an explanation. I looked at what he wrote. "Is yours the same name as that British woman detective writer?"

23   "Sort of," he answered.

24   "I like her books, although I don't read novels often." Seeing me at a loss, he asked, "How do you like the weather here?"

25   "Much the same as that in Beijing. We have cold winters, too."

26   "I hope someday I can go to Beijing."

27   "You will surely be welcome. If you wait for two years, I can show you around." I was so very eager to make a friend of him.

28   Unfortunately, the professor appeared and the class began. I would be sure to come to this class again and locate this friendly young man.

29   I didn't try my luck anymore that afternoon. Instead I found a seat in the library and tried to finish some reading assignments for Professor Thompson. I took out my books, but my mind refused to register anything. I glanced around the nearly full library; some students were doing their homework, a few were dozing° on the sofa along the wall. Looking at those tired students, I remembered an item in the campus newspaper reporting that the 1981 tuition would be $6,900. How could I blame the students for not wanting to talk to me? The costs were so high, they had to put their time and energy into their studies.

dozing: sleeping lightly

30   I put aside my books and began a letter to Fengyun,* but I couldn't finish it. Disheartened, I packed up my books and walked slowly back to my room. I knew my misery came not only from missing my family, but also from the frustration of being unable to learn. People in Beijing must be thinking I was enjoying myself here in the richest country in the world. Yet I was suffering, not because people in America were rejecting me, but because they didn't understand me and didn't seem to care how I felt—and because I didn't understand them, either. After my three classes each day, I wandered around the campus like a ghost.° I had nowhere to go.

ghost: spirit of a dead person appearing as a pale shadow

31   I felt better when dusk fell, knowing that another day had passed. ◆

*The author's wife.

3. Focused Reading

Read the text more carefully. Look for the specific strategies the author uses to meet people and to keep conversations going. With a pen or pencil, mark these in the text. Then make a list below.

1. He comes early to class.

_____

_____

_____

_____

_____

_____

HOW YOU READ

Did marking the text help you focus as you read?

4. Analyze the Story

In groups, choose one of the following to discuss. Elect a group member to report your conclusions to the class.

A. Which of the author's strategies listed above seem especially effective? Which ones have you tried or do you want to try?

B. What kind of person is the author? List three or four adjectives that describe him. Support your ideas with evidence from the text.

C. How successful is the author in his attempts at meeting people? What advice would you give him?

5. Look at Language

The author uses many words related to feeling bad. Look at the words in bold in the passage below. Study their meanings and related word forms. Then fill in the blanks in the summary.

I put aside my books and began a letter to Fengyun, but I couldn't finish it. **Disheartened,** I packed up my books and walked slowly back to my room. I knew my **misery** came not only from missing my family, but also from the **frustration** of being unable to learn. People in Beijing must be thinking I was enjoying myself here in the richest country in the world. Yet I was **suffering,** not because people in America were rejecting me, but because they didn't understand me and didn't seem to care how I felt—and because I didn't understand them, either. After my three classes each day, I wandered around the campus like a ghost. I had nowhere to go.

I felt better when dusk fell, knowing that another day had passed.

> **Feeling Bad**
> *disheartened* (adj.) depressed, unhappy, downhearted
> *misery* (n.) a condition of great suffering or pain; distress
> *miserable* (adj.) very unhappy or in pain
> *frustration* (n.) the bad feeling one gets from being unable to achieve one's objective
> *frustrate* (v.) to prevent from achieving one's objective
> *frustrated* (adj.) feeling unhappy because one cannot achieve one's objective
> *suffer* (v.) to experience pain, suffering or distress
> *suffering* (n.) a condition of pain, suffering or distress

In Chicago, Liu Zongren was often lonely, homesick, and

_____miserable_____. He tried hard to communicate with his
(miserable, frustrate,suffer)

American classmates, but when he didn't succeed, he was

_____. He _____ because
(frustration, misery, frustrated)   (disheartened, frustrated, suffered)

he felt misunderstood. His _____ was also a result of
(misery, suffer, frustrate)

missing his family. Although he was often _____
(disheartened, misery, suffer)

during the day, he felt better at night knowing that another day had

passed.

Find and circle other words in the text related to feeling bad.

6. Move Beyond the Story

Discussion

A. In your experience, what are good places to meet new friends? What are good topics to talk about with strangers or new friends? If it's possible, interview one or two Americans at your school to see how they meet new people. Share your findings with a group of classmates.

B. Liu's routine opening line for starting a conversation is "Hi. My name is Liu Zongren. I come from Beijing, China." What other opening lines can you use to meet students in your classes, the library, or the cafeteria? Fill in the bubbles.

Writing

To fight loneliness, Liu tries to meet people, he attends extra classes, he writes letters to his wife, or he wanders around the campus. What do you do to fight homesickness?

Challenge

Meet the Author

BHARATI MUKHERJEE *(born 1940)*

BHARATI MUKHERJEE was born in Calcutta, India. At the age of twenty-one she came to the United States to pursue a Ph.D. at the University of Iowa. Ms. Mukherjee is the author of several well-received and prizewinning books—novels, collections of short stories, and works of nonfiction. The following excerpt is taken from her 1975 novel *Wife*.

Ms. Mukherjee lives with her husband in California, where she teaches at the University of California at Berkeley.

1. Anticipate the Story

The following passage is from the novel *Wife*. It tells the story of Dimple Basus, a young Indian woman who, with her husband Amit, has recently come to New York City from Calcutta, India.
Find India on the map on page 181.

Dimple and her husband are renting the apartment of a couple named Mookerjis. Dimple has a serious case of homesickness.
Make some predictions about Dimple. How do you think she feels? How does she act? What does she do or not do? Write your predictions.

Find India on the map on page 181.

> **READING STRATEGY**
>
> Good readers make predictions about the content of a text before and as they read.

_____

_____

_____

_____

_____

2. Global Reading

Read the story as quickly as you can to get the main idea. Does Dimple feel or act the way you predicted?

Jot down your reactions or questions about the story here or in your journal. Share them with a partner or group.

> **HOW YOU READ**
>
> Did predicting the story help your reading? What else helped you?

🖉 **r e a d e r   r e s p o n s e**

....

....

....

....

....

....

....

....

....

....

....

Wife

◆◆

Bharati Mukherjee

STARS, DIMPLE RECALLED° HAVING READ SOMEWHERE, IMPLODE:° she felt like a star, collapsing inwardly.

recalled: remembered

implode: burst inwards

2   She stood with Amit, shoulders almost touching, and looked out on Bleecker Street from the Mookerjis' window.

3   "What's wrong?" Amit asked.

4   "Nothing," Dimple said. "It's such a nice apartment, I'm afraid I might break something or forget to water the plants."

5   "I wish we had found a place in Queens. You know, on any of the streets off Kissena Boulevard." Amit turned away from the window and tested the dryness of soil° in a potted Swedish ivy that was hanging from a basket on the wall.

soil: earth

6   The high-rise apartment on Bleecker Street was full of closets and mirrors. Marsha had emptied two closets for the Basus; the others were full of silk shirts, wool pants, suitcases with faded labels, hampers,° dusty magazines tied together with string, a scorched ironing board. Dimple spent hours going through the closets. Also drawers: she was thrilled when she found a pair of mauve°-tinted sunglasses and tried them on in the bathroom. Seeing herself in the mirror above the sink, she thought of astronauts floating in space, their faces invisible behind plastic bubbles.

hampers: large baskets with covers

mauve: a light purple

7   She wrote her mother that Amit and she had moved into a fantastic apartment belonging to N.Y.U.,° and that there were two bathrooms and bright orange shower curtains and a floral° wastebasket so pretty that she hated to throw trash in it, and a stereo and sixty-two plants (some were very small but she had to water them all) and a red rocking chair that she was afraid to sit on, and a lovely kitchen with shiny wipe-clean counter tops, a French coffee maker and Danish casseroles,° and would she please give the new address to Pixie* and tell her to write as soon as possible.

N.Y.U.: New York University

floral: flowered

casseroles: baking dishes

---

*Dimple's best friend in India.

8   She could tell Amit was happy in his job though he kept saying the job was not challenging enough and that he regarded it as a stepping-stone to something better. On their fifth evening in the Mookerjis' apartment, as she watched him make notes on the margin of *The Wall Street Journal,** she said, "The truth is I feel very tired these days. I mean, I don't have the energy to baste° the chicken every fifteen minutes, which is what the recipe calls for." Amit said, "It's probably because you eat so little." He did not look up from the paper. So she took the easy way out: she lost her temper, started to cry. She said, "I feel sort of dead inside and all you can do is read the paper and talk to me about food. You never listen; you've never listened to me. You hate me. Don't deny it; I know you do. You hate me because I'm not fat and fair."° Then she ran out of the room and picked the oven mitts° off the counter as if they were weapons, flung open the door of the oven and lunged forward.

9   "That smells divine," Amit said, standing just behind her. Standing so close, Dimple thought, that if he were to come any closer he could push her head into the oven and let it warm to 375° and serve it instead of the chicken that was cooking. "I love you; you should know that by now." Then he laughed in a self-conscious way and added, "I love you because you are a great cook. Here, let me lift that out of there."

10   She let him push her out of his way. He was wearing an extra pair of oven mitts, much fancier than hers, made up to look like bunny faces complete with button noses and calico ears. They made Amit look so absurd that she had to laugh. She was grateful that Marsha kept these weapons° to defuse° anger.

11   "There! Nothing to it!" Amit exclaimed, as he set the casserole on the table. "You just like to make a fuss."

12   "But you forgot the trivet!° The table will be scarred!"

13   The bunny mitts hopped into action, rearranging casserole and trivet. Dimple laughed so hard that her shoulders ached° and her throat felt full of mucus, as though she had been vomiting.

14   At the table, as she picked out the best parts of the chicken for Amit, she heard him say, "Boredom is the devil's workshop or however

baste: moisten with butter or drippings

fair: light in color

mitts: mittens used when cooking

weapons: instruments used in fighting and war

defuse: make less explosive

trivet: metal plate for holding hot dishes on a table

ached: hurt

*A business newspaper.

that proverb goes. The point is you must go out, make friends, do something constructive,° not stay at home and think about Calcutta."

15   Dimple recognized *constructive* as one of the words she had seen listed on the scrap of paper, along with all the other new words. She picked absent-mindedly through the wings,° neck and back and said, "I'm not brooding° about Calcutta. The trouble is, I've stopped brooding about Calcutta."

16   "Why don't you take a leg for a change?" Amit asked. "Do you think American wives always eat wings and necks like you?" Then he added that she ought to go out more often, make friends with the other women in the building—they had noticed four Indian names on the lobby register—invite them for coffee or go shopping.

17   "I want you to have the other leg tomorrow," Dimple said softly. "Anyway, I love wings." She had no idea what American wives did and had no way of finding out. How could she go up to a blond woman in the elevator and ask, peering° politely into the Grand Union shopping bag she might be clutching to her bosom,° "Excuse me, madam. Do you customarily have legs or wings?" How could she live in a country where she could not predict these basic patterns, where every other woman was a stranger, where she felt different, ignorant, exposed to ridicule° in the elevator?

18   "If I *could* brood about Calcutta I'd be okay, wouldn't I? I mean, the trouble is I'm not even dreaming about Calcutta anymore."

19   "That's a good sign," Amit said, smiling. "You're becoming American, but not too American, I hope. I don't want you to be like Mrs. Mullick and wear pants in the house!" He left the table to get a cold can of beer. He came back with the beer and a wine glass for Dimple, and poured her an inch of foam from his can. "Just this once," he begged. "It's a celebration. I mean, we have to celebrate my job and your Americanization, so go on, take a sip of beer."

20   "I couldn't," she giggled.° "It smells awful! You know I'd get sick. You want me to get sick? What's the big idea?" But she sipped the yellow beer under the foam, sipped delicately, keeping her glass high and her little finger extended outward. The wine glass made her feel knowledgeable, a little like Marsha Mookerji but more like women in commercials.°

21   "Try it, you'll like it, and it's not habit-forming."

constructive: positive, leading to improvements

wings: the forelimbs of a bird that are used for flying

brooding: thinking constantly about something

peering: looking closely

bosom: the human breast

ridicule: the act of making fun of someone

giggled: laughed (with a series of quick, high sounds)

commercials: advertisements on TV

22 "Are you absolutely sure? I won't get drunk?" She sank her lips in the foam. "It's so bitter!"°

23 "You have to get used to it, that's all. But was it true, what you said about Calcutta? I mean, are your dreams *American* now?"

24 "No, of course not," Dimple said shyly, pushing away her beer. "I was only kidding.° I'm a great kidder."

25 During the day Dimple slept, getting up only to make Amit's breakfast and put his clean clothes out on the bed and listen to his jokes (he had bought a book of jokes and was memorizing them at the rate of five a day). She had given up eating lunch; sometimes if she felt really hungry, so hungry that she couldn't stay in bed, she took leftover rice and curry° from the fridge and ate it, without warming it, straight out of the cold Freeze-Tite container. She had given up bathing during the middle of the day, an old Calcutta habit; instead she showered at night, which made her feel different and very modern. Amit had once said, "Why don't you try a sauna?° American women are supposed to love saunas. Why don't you be outgoing° like them?" But she couldn't see herself sitting naked in a very hot cubicle.° Very often, dreams woke her up, but she could not remember what they were about. If it had been Pixie dreaming, Dimple thought, the dreams would have become funny anecdotes° to tell others. She wanted to dream of Amit but she knew she would not. Amit did not feed her fantasy life; he was merely the provider of small material comforts. In bitter moments she ranked husband, blender, color TV, cassette tape recorder, stereo, in their order of convenience.

26 There were no letters from Pixie, just a UNICEF card in mid-September saying, "Hi, Dimple old girl. Greetings from your forgotten friends in good old Cal!° Long time no scribble.° How come?° Here's hoping you'll sharpen your epistolary gifts.° Affly, Pixie." She did not get around to answering the card. Every day she thought she should write a letter, something funny and witty with little hints of how American she had become but not so American that she was ridiculous, but every day she kept putting it off.° It was too much effort to take an aerogramme out of the big shoebox in the bedroom closet where Amit kept them (he had started to take care of all correspondence in the family), think of funny things she had done or seen and put them in words. The words were never right, she thought, because she had not

bitter: having a sharp and unpleasant taste

kidding: joking

curry: a stew typical of the East Indies

sauna: a steam bath originating in Finland

outgoing: sociable, friendly

cubicle: a very small room

anecdotes: stories

Cal: Calcutta

Long time no scribble: It has been a long time since you've written

How come: Why

epistolary gifts: letter-writing talents

putting it off: postponing it until later

seen or done anything since coming to the States except sleep and cook. Some mornings, she held her head stiffly on the pillow so she would not be distracted° by the pink and lilac flowers on the pillowcase, stared at the ceiling, and tried out beginnings for the eventual letter:

27   My dear Pixie: How I wish I were in Cal with you. I do miss the hustle and bustle.°. . .

28   But *wish* and *miss* were wrong. She was not missing Calcutta really, though it would have been nice to wear new saris° and go to the Skyroom and order iced coffee. It was something else, like knowing that if she were to go out the front door, down the elevator (she was frightened by self-service elevators with their red Emergency buttons and wished there were a liftman on a stool to press the right buttons for her), if she were to stand in the lobby and say to the first ten people she saw, "Do you know it's almost October and Durga Pujah* is coming?" they would think she was mad.° She could not live with people who didn't understand about *Durga Pujah.* ◆

distracted: diverted, confused

hustle and bustle: noisy, hurried activity

saris: garments worn by Hindu women

mad: crazy

---

*An annual Hindu festival.

3. Focused Reading

What are the signs of Dimple's homesickness? In other words, what unusual things does she do (or not do) that show her unhappiness in New York? Fill in the blanks as you reread.

She spends a lot of time looking through ___closets___ .

She doesn't have much ___energy___ .

She loses her _____ and cries easily.

She overreacts to things _____ says and does.

She doesn't _____ the apartment often.

She doesn't _____ friends.

She sleeps during the _____ .

She stops eating _____ .

She can't write _____ .

_____ (other)

_____ (other)

Discuss your answers with a partner.

4. Analyze the Story

In groups, choose one of the following to discuss. Elect a group member to report your conclusions to the class.

A. Is Dimple a likeable character, in your opinion? Why or why not?

B. Compare Dimple and Amit's reactions to life in New York City. Do they react differently? How? Why?

C. Talk about the meaning of the last line of the story: "She could not live with people who didn't understand about *Durga Pujah*."

5. Look at Language

There are many two-word verbs such as **look out** *and* **turn away** *in this text. Two-word verbs are a combination of verb + preposition. Try to put the correct preposition in the sentences below. Check your answers with a partner first, and then look back at the text.*

1. "[Dimple] was thrilled when she found a pair of mauve-tinted sunglasses and tried them _____ in the bathroom. Seeing herself in the mirror above the sink, she thought _____ astronauts floating in space, their faces invisible behind plastic bubbles."

in
up
to
of
on
for
out
off
around

2. "'The truth is I feel very tired these days. I mean, I don't have the energy to baste the chicken every fifteen minutes, which is what the recipe calls _____.' Amit said, 'It's probably because you eat so little.' He did not look _____ from the paper."

3. "During the day Dimple slept, getting _____ only to make Amit's breakfast and put his clean clothes _____ on the bed and listen _____ his jokes (he had bought a book of jokes and was memorizing them at the rate of five a day). She had given _____ eating lunch. . . ."

4. "She did not get _____ to answering the card. Every day she thought she should write a letter, something funny and witty with little hints of how American she had become but not so American that she was ridiculous, but every day she kept putting it _____ . It was too much effort to take an aerogramme _____ of the big shoebox in the bedroom closet where Amit kept them (he had started to take care _____ all correspondence in the family), think _____ funny things she had done or seen and put them in words."

6. Move Beyond the Story

Discussion

Durga Pujah is obviously a very important holiday for Dimple. Find out about other important holidays around the world. Interview some of your classmates about their favorite holidays. Fill out the chart.

Classmate's Name	Favorite Holiday	What Do People Do on This Holiday?

Writing

A. Write a short summary of the story.

B. Compare Dimple and Mamacita, from No Speak English. How are they similar?

C. Dimple is unable to write a letter to her best friend, Pixie. Can you help her? Imagine you are Dimple; write a letter from your heart.

UNIT 3 ◆ *Review*

◆◆◆◆◆◆◆◆◆◆◆◆◆◆◆◆◆◆◆◆◆◆◆◆◆◆◆◆◆◆◆◆◆◆◆◆

Texts	Main Characters
NO SPEAK ENGLISH	Mamacita Mamacita's husband
TWO YEARS IN THE MELTING POT	the author, Liu Zongren
WIFE	Dimple Dimple's husband, Amit

Work individually, with a partner, or with a group to complete one of these tasks.

1. Take a class survey. Ask: **Which story did you like best? Why?** Post your results on a bulletin board.

2. Tell which character you identify with most. Why? If you wish, take a class survey on the question and post the results.

3. Think about Mamacita's marriage and Dimple's marriage. Are they alike in any way?

4. Compare a character in one story with a character from another. What do they have in common? How are they different?

Changing

The poems and the story in this unit are about changing. Have you changed since arriving in this country? How? Are the changes all positive ones? In your journal, write about these questions.

79

Meet the Author

VIRGINIA CERENIO

VIRGINIA CERENIO was born in California. She is a second-generation Filipino American. Both her parents immigrated from the Philippines. She has published a collection of poetry as well as poems in various anthologies. The following poem was published in 1989 in the anthology *The Forbidden Stitch*.

Ms. Cerenio lives in San Francisco, California, where she writes poetry and runs her own transportation company.

1. Anticipate the Poem

Find the Philippines on the map on page 181. Look at the title of this poem and read the first two lines. What do you think the poem will describe?

_____

_____

_____

_____

_____

2. Global Reading

As you read the poem the first time, cover the glossed terms. Try to guess at the meaning of the new words. Try to form a general picture in your mind as you read.

Jot down your reactions or questions about the poem here or in your journal. Share them with a partner or group.

reader response

....

....

....

....

....

....

....

....

....

....

....

....

Family Photos: Black and White: 1960

◆◆

Virginia Cerenio

the light slides through lace panels on the window
on the dark sofa sit two children
the baby propped up like a five-pound rice sack°   sack: bag
leaning against a little girl.
5 she smiles, the white curve of baby teeth   bangs: a fringe of hair
a geometric contrast to her straight china doll bangs.°   on the forehead
the father stands with a slight° smile   slight: small
in pinstriped suit, hand on hip
his hair shiny with pomade
10 three flowers or brilliantine°   three flowers,
a handkerchief points out of his breast pocket   brilliantine: brand names
even though you cannot see his shoes   of hair pomade
you know they are polished.
the mother, young and plump, from eating
15 american food: candy bars, baked potatoes
she sits in a flowered dress
hair marcelled in waves°   marcelled in waves:
her face open and full   curled carefully
no longer the shy village beauty
20 she crosses her legs casually°   casually: carelessly, as if
and laughs at the photographer   by chance
she hopes her mother in the philippines
will be very proud.

3. Focused Reading

Read the poem again for more details about the photo. Try to sketch it here.

Show a partner your sketch. How are your sketches similar or different?

4. Analyze the Poem

In groups, choose one of the following to discuss. Elect a group member to report your conclusions to the class.

A. How has the woman in the photograph changed since leaving the Philippines? Find at least five changes.

B. Underline words or phrases in the poem that describe the body language of the woman and her husband. Would their poses be different if they had never left their country? Will the woman's mother approve?

C. Look at the last two lines of the poem. How will the woman's mother react to the photo? Will she be proud?

5. Look at Language

A. *This poem paints a picture by using many descriptive adjectives. Fill in the blanks below with an adjective. Check your choices by looking back at the poem on page 82.*

Family Photos: Black and White: 1960

the light slides through lace panels on the window

on the dark sofa sit two children

the baby propped up like a five-pound rice sack

5   leaning against a little girl.

she smiles, the white curve of baby teeth

a geometric contrast to her _____ china doll bangs.

the father stands with a _____ smile

in _____ suit, hand on hip

10   his hair _____ with pomade

three flowers or brilliantine

a handkerchief points out of his breast pocket

even though you cannot see his shoes

you know they are _____ .

15   the mother, young and _____ , from eating

american food: candy bars, baked potatoes

she sits in a _____ dress

hair marcelled in waves

her face _____ and full

20   no longer the shy village beauty

she crosses her legs casually

and laughs at the photographer

she hopes her mother in the philippines

will be very proud.

flowered
polished
straight
open
shiny
pinstriped
slight
plump

B. Underline three descriptions of hair in the poem. Then write a
    complete description of your hair. All of the words in the
    illustration are adjectives unless otherwise noted.

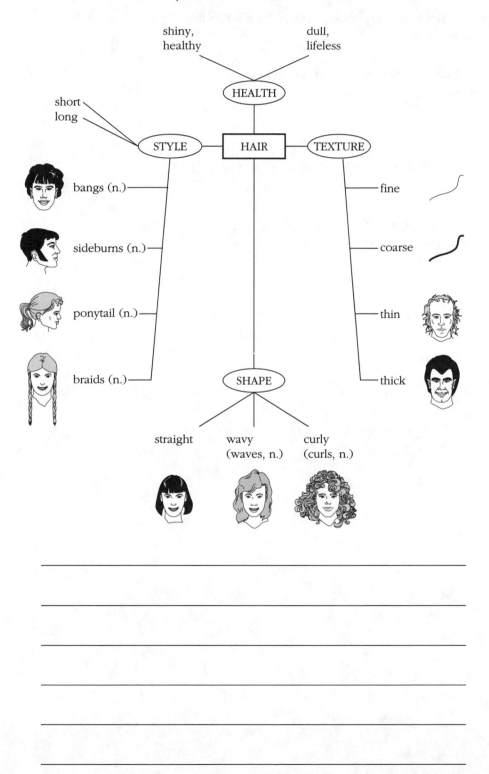

_____

_____

_____

_____

_____

_____

6. Move Beyond the Poem

Discussion

A. Have you changed since leaving your country? How? Are the changes good or bad?

B. Did you like the poem? Why or why not? What is your favorite word, phrase, or sentence?

Writing

A. Look at a photo of yourself or your family. Describe it in poetry or prose.

B. Write a letter to the author about the poem. Ask any questions you have. Send it to the author at 530 Bacon St., San Francisco, CA 94134.

Meet the Author

VICTOR HERNANDEZ CRUZ *(born 1949)*

VICTOR HERNANDEZ CRUZ was born in Puerto Rico. In 1954, when he was five years old, his family moved to New York City. But the family kept its island traditions. Hernandez Cruz remembers, "My family's life was full of music—guitars, conga drums, and songs. My mother sang songs. Even when it was five degrees below zero in New York she sang warm tropical ballads." Mr. Hernandez Cruz published his first collection of poetry to rave reviews when he was just twenty years old. The following poem comes from his 1973 collection, *Mainland*.

Mr. Hernandez Cruz lives in Aguas Buenas, Puerto Rico.

1. Anticipate the Poem

What do you know about Puerto Rico? How is it different from New York? Find it on the map on page 180.

The following poem is about a Puerto Rican man who comes to live in New York. (He is one of nearly 900,000 Puerto Ricans in New York.) He has brought a bag of mango seeds with him.

Read the first nine lines of the poem. With the class, talk about possible reasons why the man has brought mango seeds with him.

_____

_____

_____

_____

_____

READING STRATEGY

Good readers don't stop at a new word. They continue reading and try to understand it from the context. Stopping to look up words can result in losing the main idea of the text.

2. Global Reading

Read the poem through without stopping to use your dictionary. Think about these questions as you read:

　　What happens to the seed?

　　What happens to the man?

Jot down any reactions or questions you have about the poem here or in your journal. Share them with a partner or group.

 HOW YOU READ

Did you enjoy reading this? Why or why not?

reader response

....

....

....

....

....

....

....

....

....

....

....

The Man Who Came to the Last Floor

◆◆◆◆◆◆◆◆◆◆◆◆◆◆◆◆◆◆◆◆◆◆◆◆◆◆◆◆◆◆◆◆

Victor Hernandez Cruz

There was a Puerto Rican man who
came to New York
He came with a whole shopping bag
full of seeds° strange to the big
city
He came and it was morning
and though many people thought the
sun was out this man wondered:
"Where is it"
"Y el sol donde esta"* he asked
himself
He went to one of the neighborhoods
and searched for an apartment
He found one in the large somewhere
of New York
with a window overlooking a busy avenue
It was the kind of somewhere that is
usually elevatorless
Somewhere near wall/less
stairless
But this man enjoyed the wide space
of the room with the window that
overlooked the avenue
There was plenty of space
looking out of the window
There is a direct path to heaven°
he thought
A wideness in front of the living
room

seeds: the part of a plant from which new plants will grow

heaven: the space around the earth; where God exists

---

*Spanish for "And where is the sun?"

It was the sixth floor so he lived
on top of everybody in the building
The last floor of the mountain
He took to° staring out of his sixth
floor window
He was a familiar sight every day
From his window he saw legs that
walked all day
Short and skinny fat legs
Legs that belonged to many people
Legs that walk embraced with nylon socks
Legs that ride bareback°
Legs that were swifter° than others
Legs that were always hiding
Legs that always had to turn around
and look at the horizon°
Legs that were just legs against
the grey of the cement
People with no legs
He saw everything hanging out
from his room
Big city anywhere and his smile
was as wide as the space in front of him

2 One day his dreams were invaded by spirits°
People just saw him change
Change the way rice changes when it is
sitting on top of fire
All kinds of things started to happen
at the top of the mountain
Apartamento number 32
All kinds of smells started to come out
of apartamento number 32
All kinds of visitors started to come
to apartamento number 32
Wild looking ladies showed up
with large earrings and bracelets
that jingled° throughout the hallways

took to: started to

bareback: on a horse with no saddle

swifter: faster

horizon: the line where the sky seems to meet the earth

spirits: supernatural beings (ghosts, angels, demons, etc.)

jingled: made light, ringing sounds

The neighborhood became rich in legend°
One could write an encyclopedia if one
collected the rumors°
But nothing bothered this man who was
on top of everybody's heads
He woke one day and put the shopping bag
full of seeds that he brought from the island
near the window
He said "para que aproveche el fresco"*
So that it can enjoy the fresh air
He left it there for a day
Taking air
Fresh air
Grey air
Wet air
The avenue air
The blue legs air
The teen-agers who walked below
Their air
With their black hats with the red
bandana around them full of cocaine°
That air
The heroin° in the young girls that
moved slowly toward their local
high school
All the air from the outside
The shopping bag stood by the window
inhaling°
Police air
Bus air
Car wind
Gringo† air
Big mountain city air anywhere

legend: an important story passed from one generation to the next

rumors: gossip; unconfirmed stories

cocaine: a habit-forming drug made from dried coca leaves

heroin: a habit-forming drug derived from morphine

inhaling: breathing in

---

*Spanish for "so that it can enjoy the fresh air."
†A Latin American word for "North American."

That day this man from Puerto Rico
had his three radios on at the same time
Music coming from anywhere
Each station was different
Music from anywhere everywhere

3   The following day the famous
    outline of the man's head once again showed
    up on the sixth floor window
    This day he fell into song
    and his head was in motion
    No one recalls° exactly at what point

recalls: remembers

    in the song he started flinging° the

flinging: throwing

    seeds of tropical fruits down to
    the earth
    Down to the avenue of somewhere big
    city
    But no one knew what he was doing
    So all the folks just smiled
    "El hombre esta bien loco, algo le
    cogio la cabeza"*
    The man is really crazy
    something has taken his head
    He began to throw out the last of the
    Mango° seeds

mango: a yellow-red
tropical fruit

    A policeman was walking down the avenue
    and all of a sudden took off his hat
    A mango seed landed nicely into his
    curly hair
    It somehow sailed into the man's
    scalp°

scalp: the skin on the top
of the head

    Deep into the grease of his curls
    No one saw it
    And the policeman didn't feel it
    He put his hat on and walked away

_____

*Spanish for "the man is really crazy, something has taken his head."

The man from Puerto Rico
was singing another pretty song
His eyes were closed and his head waved.

4 Two weeks later the policeman felt
a bump coming out of his head
"Holy smokes"° he woke up telling his wife
one day
"this bump is getting so big I can't
put my hat on my head"
He took a day off and went to see his
doctor about his growing bump
The doctor looked at it and said
it'll go away
The bump didn't go away
It went toward the sky
getting bigger each day
It began to take hold of his whole head
Every time he tried to comb his hair
all his hair would fall to the comb
One morning when the sun was really hot
his wife noticed a green leaf sticking
out from the tip of his bump
Another month passed and more and more
leaves started to show on this man's head
Surely he was going crazy he thought
He could not go to work with a mango
tree growing out of his head
It soon got to be five feet tall
and beautifully green
He had to sleep in the living room
His bedroom could no longer contain him
Weeks later a young mango showed up
hanging from a newly formed branch
"Now look at this" he told his wife
He had to drink a lot of water or he'd
get severe headaches

holy smokes: an expression of surprise (slang)

The more water he drank the bigger
the mango tree flourished over his head
The people of the somewhere city heard
about it in the evening news and there was
a line of thousands ringed around his
home
They all wanted to see the man who
had an exotic mango tree growing from
his skull
And there was nothing that could be done.

5   Everyone was surprised when they
saw the man who lived at the top of
the mountain come down with his shopping
bag and all his luggage
He told a few of his friends that
he was going back to Puerto Rico
When they asked him why he was going back
He told them that he didn't remember
ever leaving
He said that his wife and children
were there waiting for him
The other day he noticed that he was
not on his island he said
almost singing
He danced toward the famous corner
and waved down a taxi
"El Aire port" he said
He was going to the clouds
To the island
At the airport he picked up a newspaper
and was reading an article about a mango
tree
At least that's what he could make out of
the English
Que cosa* he said   Wao

---

*Spanish for "What is this?"

Why write about a Mango tree
There're so many of them
and they are everywhere
They taste goooooood
Como eh.* ◆

---

*Spanish for "And how."

3. Focused Reading

The man from Puerto Rico changes in New York. People say he is going crazy. As you read again, mark the lines that show his strange behavior. Then fill in the boxes.

☞ **HOW YOU READ**

Did marking the text help you focus as you read?

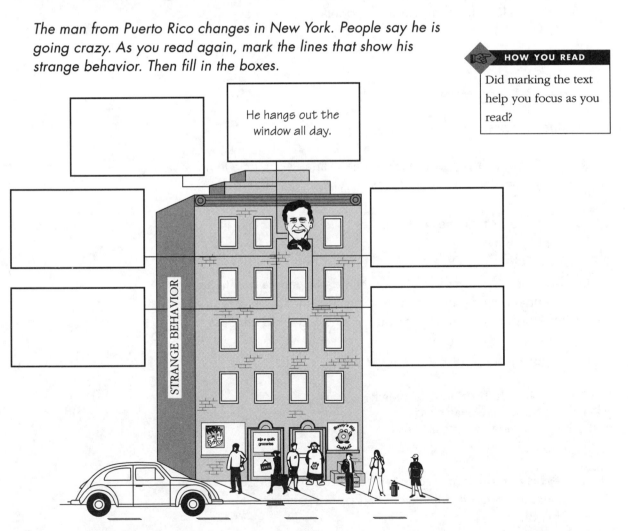

He hangs out the window all day.

STRANGE BEHAVIOR

4. Analyze the Poem

In groups, choose one of the following to discuss. Elect a group member to report your conclusions to the class.

A. Why did the man from Puerto Rico leave New York?

B. When the man returned to Puerto Rico, he left a mango tree behind. Why a mango tree? What does it represent? What is significant about where it grew?

C. What do we see of life in New York City through the man's window? Make a list of as many things as you can. What can you conclude from this about the poet's point of view on New York?

5. Look at Language

Do one or more of these activities.

A. Find words or phrases that are often repeated. Circle them. Why does the poet repeat these? What is the effect?

B. Find one or two lines in the poem that you especially like. Explain why.

C. There is a lot of movement and motion of people and things in the poem. Underline words and phrases that show movement. What is the poet trying to convey by using these images?

D. In paragraph 1 of the poem, we read

> It was the kind of somewhere that is
> usually elevatorless
> Somewhere near wall/less
> stairless

Less is a suffix that means "without." It can be added to some nouns to form an adjective. The opposite suffix, *-ful,* means "full of."

Make two new adjectives from each of the nouns below.

Nouns	Adjective with *-less*	Adjective with *-ful*
joy	joyless	joyful
fear		
hope		
pain		
taste		
use		
purpose		
fruit		
care		
mercy		
color		
harm		

6. Move Beyond the Poem

Discussion

A. Mango seeds and mango trees seem, for the poet, to be closely associated with his native land, Puerto Rico. Write or draw three objects that, for you, represent the essence of your country. Share your ideas with a group. Tell why these objects are important to you.

B. Does living in a new country change people? How has it changed you? How has it changed other people you know who have come from your native country to North America?

Do immigrants to North America change their new country? Think of five specific contributions that immigrant groups have made to North America.

Writing

A. Write a short reaction to the poem. Tell your opinion or feelings about it and what it makes you think of.

B. In paragraph 1 of the poem, the poet describes the many different kinds of legs that the man from Puerto Rico sees as he looks out his window:

> From his window he saw legs that
> walked all day
> Short and skinny fat legs
> Legs that belonged to many people
> Legs that walk embraced with nylon socks
> Legs that ride bareback
> Legs that were swifter than others
> Legs that were always hiding

Look out your window. What do you see? Legs? Faces? Heads? Buildings? Cars? Trees? Choose one category and describe the variety that you see in poem form.

C. Write a letter to the poet telling your impressions of the poem and asking any questions you have. Send it to him c/o Arte Público Press, University of Houston, Houston, TX 77204-2090.

Challenge

Meet the Author

JUDITH ORTIZ COFER *(born 1952)*

JUDITH ORTIZ COFER was born in Puerto Rico. She spent her childhood going back and forth between the warm island of her birth and New Jersey. The following autobiographical story comes from her award-winning *Silent Dancing* (1990), a remembrance of her childhood.

About her writing, Ms. Cofer says, "As a native Puerto Rican, my first language was Spanish. It was a challenge, not only to learn English, but to master it enough to write poetry in it—my ultimate goal."

Ms. Cofer lives with her family in Georgia.

1. Anticipate the Story

In Judith Ortiz Cofer's memoir, *Silent Dancing*, she remembers her childhood, when she moved back and forth between Puerto Rico and New Jersey. In the following true story, "Vida," the author describes a fascinating Chilean girl who lived above her in New Jersey and changed her life.

Find Chile on the map on page 180. When you were a child or young teen, was there someone who had a powerful influence on you? Tell a partner about this person.

_____

_____

_____

_____

READING STRATEGY

Some readers like to mark a text as they read. They underline important parts, write comments in the margins, or put question marks next to parts they don't understand. This helps them interact with the text.

2. Global Reading

As you read, try to form a general picture of Vida as a person. Try marking the text to help you focus as you read.

Jot down your reactions or questions about the story here or in your journal. Share them with a partner or group.

HOW YOU READ

Did marking the text help you focus as you read?

reader response

....
....
....
....
....
....
....
....
....
....
....

Vida

◆◆

Judith Ortiz Cofer

VIDA WAS A BEAUTIFUL CHILEAN GIRL who appeared in the apartment upstairs with her refugee family one day and introduced herself into our daily drama.

2   She was tall, thin and graceful as a ballerina, with fair skin and short black hair. She looked like a gazelle° as she bounded down the stairs from her apartment to ours the day she first came to our door to borrow something. Her accent charmed us. She said that she had just arrived from Chile with her sister, her sister's newborn baby girl, her sister's husband, and their grandmother. They were all living together in a one-bedroom apartment on the floor above us.

gazelle: a fast, graceful antelope with large eyes

3   There must have been an interesting story of political exile there, but I was too young to care about that detail. I was immediately fascinated by the lovely Vida who looked like one of the models in the fashion magazines that I, just turning twelve, had begun to be interested in. Vida came into my life during one of my father's long absences with the Navy, so that his constant vigilance° was not a hindrance° to my developing attachment to this vibrant° human being. It was not a friendship—she was too much older than I and too self-involved to give me much in return for my devotion. It was more a Sancho Panza/Knight of La Mancha* relationship, with me following her while she explored the power of her youth and beauty.

vigilance: watchfulness

hindrance: obstacle, something in the way

vibrant: energetic, alive

4   Vida wanted to be a movie star in Hollywood. That is why she had come to America, she said. I believed that she would be, although she spoke almost no English. That was my job, she said, to teach her to speak perfect English without an accent. She had finished secondary school in her country, and although she was only sixteen, she was not going to school in Paterson. She had other plans. She would get a job as soon as she had papers, save money, then she would leave for Hollywood as soon as possible. She asked me how far Hollywood was. I showed her the state of California in my geography book. She traced a

---

*Sancho Panza is the simple peasant accompanying the hero Don Quixote (also known as Knight of La Mancha) in Cervantes' fifteenth-century romance.

line with her finger from New Jersey to the west coast and smiled. Nothing seemed impossible to Vida.

5   It was summer when I met Vida, and we spent our days in the small, fenced-in square lot behind our apartment building, avoiding going indoors as much as possible, since it was depressing to Vida to hear her family talking about the need to find jobs, to smell sour baby smells, or to be constantly lectured to by her obese° grandmother who sat like a great pile of laundry on a couch all day, watching shows on television which she did not understand. The brother-in-law frightened me a little with his intense eyes and his constant pacing.° He spoke in whispers to his wife, Vida's sister, when I was around, as if he did not want me to overhear important matters, making me feel like an intruder.° I didn't like to look at Vida's sister. She looked like a Vida who had been left out in the elements° for too long: skin stuck to the bones. Vida did not like her family either. When I asked, she said that her mother was dead and that she did not want to speak of the past. Vida thought of only the future.

6   Once, when we were alone in her apartment, she asked me if I wanted to see her in a bathing suit. She went into the bathroom and emerged in a tight red one-piece suit. She reclined on the bed in a pose she had obviously seen in a magazine. "Do you think I am beautiful?" she asked me. I answered yes, suddenly overwhelmed by a feeling of hopelessness for my skinny° body, bony arms and legs, flat chest. "Cadaverous,"° Vida had once whispered, smiling wickedly into my face after taking my head into her hands and feeling my skull° so close to the surface. But right afterwards she had kissed my cheek reassuring me that I would "flesh out"° in a few years.

7   That summer my life shifted on its axis.° Until Vida, my mother had been the magnetic force around which all my actions revolved. Since my father was away for long periods of time, my young mother and I had developed a strong symbiotic relationship,° with me playing the part of interpreter° and buffer° to the world for her. I knew at an early age that I would be the one to face landlords, doctors, store clerks, and other "strangers" whose services we needed in my father's absence. English was my weapon and my power. As long as she lived in her fantasy that her exile from Puerto Rico was temporary and that she did not need to learn the language, keeping herself "pure" for her

obese: very fat

pacing: walking back and forth

intruder: someone entering private property uninvited

the elements: wind, rain, sun, etc.

skinny: very thin

cadaverous: like a cadaver (dead body)

skull: the bones that make up the head

flesh out: grow fatter

shifted on its axis: changed direction

symbiotic relationship: in biology, the close association of two dissimilar organisms, where there are advantages for both

interpreter: translator

buffer: something that lessens a shock or conflict

return to the Island, then I was in control of our lives outside the realm of our little apartment in Paterson—that is, until Father came home from his Navy tours: then the mantle of responsibility would fall on him. At times, I resented° his homecomings, when I would suddenly be thrust back into the role of dependent which I had long ago outgrown—and not by choice.

8   But Vida changed me. I became secretive, and every outing from our apartment building—to get my mother a pack of L&M's*; to buy essentials at the drugstore or supermarket . . . ; and, Vida's favorite, to buy Puerto Rican groceries at the *bodega*†—became an adventure with Vida. She was getting restless° living in such close quarters with her paranoid° sister and brother-in-law. The baby's crying and the pervasive smells of dirty diapers° drove her crazy as well as her fat grandmother's lethargy° disturbed only by the old woman's need to lecture Vida about her style of dress and her manners, which even my mother had started to comment on.

9   Vida was modeling herself on the Go-Go girls she loved to watch on dance shows on our television set. She would imitate their movements with me as her audience until we both fell on the sofa laughing. Her eye make-up (bought with my allowance)° was dark and heavy, her lips were glossy with iridescent tan lipstick, and her skirts were riding higher and higher on her long legs. When we walked up the street on one of my errands, the men stared; the Puerto Rican men did more than that. More than once we were followed by men inspired to compose *piropos* for Vida—erotically° charged words spoken behind us in stage whispers.°

10   I was scared and excited by the trail of Vida's admirers. It was a dangerous game for both of us, but for me especially, since my father could come home unannounced at any time and catch me at it. I was the invisible° partner in Vida's life; I was her little pocket mirror she could take out any time to confirm her beauty and her power. But I was too young to think in those terms, all I knew was the thrill of being in

resented: felt unhappy about

restless: uneasy, wanting change

paranoid: mentally unbalanced by delusions

diapers: undergarments worn by babies

lethargy: a lack of energy

allowance: a small amount of money given regularly to a child

erotically: sexually

stage whispers: loud whispers, as would happen on a theater stage

invisible: that cannot be seen

*A brand name of cigarettes.
†Spanish for "food market."

her company, being touched by her magical powers of transformation that could make a walk to the store a deliciously sinful escapade.

11   Then Vida fell in love. He was, in my jealous eyes, a Neanderthal,* a big hairy man who drove a large black Oldsmobile recklessly around our block hour after hour just to catch a glimpse of° Vida. He had promised to drive her to California, she confided to me. Then she started to use me as cover° in order to meet him, asking me to take a walk with her, then leaving me to wait on a park bench or at the library for what seemed an eternity while she drove around with her muscle-bound lover. I became disenchanted° with Vida, but remained loyal to her throughout the summer. Once in a while we still shared a good time. She loved to tell me in detail about her "romance." Apparently, she was not totally naive,° and had managed to keep their passionate encounters within the limits of kissing and petting° in the spacious backseat of the black Oldsmobile. But he was getting impatient, she told me, so she had decided to announce her engagement to her family soon. They would get married and go to California together. He would be her manager and protect her from the Hollywood "wolves."

12   By this time I was getting weary° of Vida's illusions° about Hollywood. I was glad when school started in the fall and I got into my starched blue jumper only to discover that it was too tight and too short for me. I had "developed" over the summer.

13   Life settled to our normal routine when we were in the States. This was: my brother and I went to Catholic school and did our lessons, our mother waited for our father to come home on leave from his Navy tours, and all of us waited to hear when we would be returning to Puerto Rico—which was usually every time Father went to Europe, every six months or so. Vida would sometimes come down to our apartment and complain bitterly about life with her family upstairs. They had absolutely refused to accept her fiancé.° They were making plans to migrate elsewhere. She did not have work papers yet, but did not want to go with them. She would have to find a place to stay until she got married. She began courting° my mother. I would come home to find them looking at bride magazines and laughing together. Vida hardly spoke to me at all.

catch a glimpse of: get a quick look at

cover: a screen or protection

disenchanted: disappointed

naive: innocent, childlike

petting: embracing and touching (colloquial)

weary: tired

illusions: unreal or false ideas or beliefs

fiancé: the man that a woman plans to marry

courting: trying to win the love of

---

*A prehistoric race of people.

14   Father came home in his winter blues° and everything changed for us. I felt the almost physical release of the burden of responsibility for my family and allowed myself to spend more time doing what I like to do best of all—read. It was a solitary° life we led in Paterson, New Jersey, and both my brother and I became avid readers. . . .The ebb and flow° of this routine was interrupted by Vida that year. With my mother's help she introduced herself into our family.

15   Father, normally a reticent° man, suspicious of strangers by nature, and always vigilant about dangers to his children, also fell under Vida's spell.° Amazingly, he agreed to let her come stay in our apartment until her wedding some months away. She moved into my room. She slept on what had been my little brother's twin bed until he got his own room, a place where I liked to keep my collection of dolls from around the world that my father had sent me. These had to be put in a box in the dark closet now.

16   Vida's perfume took over my room. As soon as I walked in, I smelled her. It got on my clothes. The nuns° at my school commented on it since we were not allowed to use perfume or cosmetics. I tried to wash it off, but it was strong and pervasive. Vida tried to win me by taking me shopping. She was getting money from her boyfriend—for her trousseau°—she said. She bought me a tight black skirt just like hers and a pair of shoes with heels. When she had me model it for my family, my father frowned° and left the room silently. I was not allowed to keep the things. Since the man was never seen at our house, we did not know that Vida had broken the engagement and was seeing other men.

17   My mother started to complain about little things Vida did, or did not do. She did not help with housework, although she did contribute money. Where was she getting it? She did not bathe daily (a major infraction° in my mother's eyes), but poured cologne over herself in quantities. She claimed to be at church too many times a week and came home smelling of alcohol, even though it was hard to tell because of the perfume. Mother was spreading her wings° and getting ready to fight for exclusivity° over her nest.°

18   But, Father, surprising us all again, argued for fairness for the *señorita*—my mother made a funny "harrump" noise at that word, which in Spanish connotes virginity and purity. He said we had promised her asylum° until she got settled and it was important that we send her out of our house in a respectable manner: married, if possible.

winter blues: blue winter navy uniform

solitary: lonely

ebb and flow: a back and forth movement (usually of the sea)

reticent: silent, uncommunicative

spell: magical power

nuns: members of a female Catholic religious order

trousseau: a bride's collection of clothes, linen, etc.

frowned: turned (his) mouth down at the corners

infraction: a breaking of the law

wings: the forelimbs of a bird used for flying

exclusivity: the excluding or keeping out of others

nest: the place where birds keep their young

asylum: a place of safety

He liked playing cards with her. She was cunning and smart, a worthy adversary.°

19   Mother fumed.° My brother and I spent a lot of time in the kitchen or living room, reading where the air was not saturated with "Evening in Paris."*

20   Vida was changing. After a few months, she no longer spoke of Hollywood; she barely spoke to me at all. She got her papers and got a job in a factory sewing dungarees.° Then, almost as suddenly as she had come into my life, she disappeared.

21   One afternoon I came home to find my mother mopping the floors strenuously with a pine cleaner, giving the apartment the kind of thorough scrubbing usually done as a family effort in the spring. When I went into my room the dolls were back in their former place on the extra bed. No sign of Vida.

22   I don't remember discussing her parting° much. Although my parents were fair, they did not always feel the need to explain or justify their decisions to us. I have always believed that my mother simply demanded her territory, fearing the growing threat° of Vida's beauty and erotic slovenliness° that was permeating° her clean home. Or perhaps Vida found life with us as stifling° as she had with her family. If I had been a little older, I would have learned more from Vida, but she came at a time when I needed security more than knowledge of human nature. She was a fascinating creature.

23   The last time I saw Vida's face it was on a poster. It announced her crowning as a beauty queen for a Catholic church in another parish. Beauty contests were held by churches as fundraisers° at that time, as contradictory as that seems to me now: a church sponsoring a competition to choose the most physically attractive female in the congregation. I still feel that it was right to see Vida wearing the little tiara of fake diamonds in that photograph with the caption underneath: *Vida wins!* ◆

adversary: enemy

fumed: showed anger

dungarees: blue jeans

parting: leaving

threat: an indication or expression of danger

slovenliness: dirtiness

permeating: going into and spreading through

stifling: suffocating, lacking fresh air

fundraisers: social events that collect money for a worthy cause

---

*A brand name of perfume.

3. Focused Reading

Vida is an agent of change in the story. As you reread, think about Vida's actions. What effect do her actions have on the author and the author's family? Fill in the boxes. Discuss your conclusions with a partner.

Vida's Actions	Changes in the Author's Life
1. Vida arrives from Chile with her dreams of Hollywood.	The author starts to spend a lot of time away from her family. She becomes secretive and increasingly aware of her own sexuality.
2. Vida falls in love.	_____ _____
3. Vida courts the author's mother.	_____ _____
4. Vida's behavior in the author's home begins to bother everyone but the author's father.	_____ _____
5. Vida leaves.	_____ _____

4. Analyze the Story

In groups, choose one of the following to discuss. Elect a group member to report your conclusions to the class.

A. Vida brought change into other people's lives. But in this story she changed too. How?

B. The author eventually lost her illusions about Vida. What habits and behavior did Vida have that the author did not approve of?

C. Why did the author's mother want Vida out of their home?

5. Look at Language

Literary language often uses comparisons to help readers get a clear picture. **Similes** (1 and 2 below) are explicit comparisons that use **as** or **like**. **Metaphors** (3 and 4) are implicit comparisons in which a person or thing is presented as something else.

1. "[Vida] was tall, thin and graceful *as a ballerina*. . . ."

2. "I was immediately fascinated by the lovely Vida who looked *like one of the models in the fashion magazines*. . . ."

3. "English was *my weapon*. . . ."

4. "Mother was *spreading her wings* and getting ready to fight for exclusivity over her *nest*."

Complete these similes and metaphors from "Vida." Look back at the text to check your answers. Which comparison do you like best? Why?

an intruder	a gazelle
a Neanderthal	the magnetic force
a great pile of laundry	her little pocket mirror

1. "[Vida] looked like _____ as she bounded down the stairs from her apartment to ours." (paragraph 2)

2. "[It] was depressing to Vida . . . to be constantly lectured to by her obese grandmother who sat like _____ on the couch all day. . . ." (paragraph 5)

3. "He spoke in whispers to his wife, Vida's sister, when I was around, as if he did not want me to overhear important matters, making me feel like _____ ." (paragraph 5)

4. "Until Vida, my mother had been _____ around which all my actions revolved." (paragraph 7)

5. "I was the invisible partner in Vida's life; I was _____ she could take out any time to confirm her beauty and her power." (paragraph 10)

6. "Then Vida fell in love. He was, in my jealous eyes, _____ , a big hairy man who drove a large black Oldsmobile. . . ." (paragraph 11)

6. Move Beyond the Story

Discussion

A. Vida had dreams of becoming a Hollywood movie star when she came to the United States. She eventually got a job at a factory. Discuss the "American dream." What does it mean to you? Is it still possible to achieve in today's economic climate?

B. Choose a character and situation below to role-play. Tell "your friends" (other group members) how you feel.

1. Vida: arriving in the United States
2. The author: right after meeting Vida
3. Vida: getting a job at the factory
4. The author: right after Vida moved out
5. The author's mother: right after Vida moved out

Writing

A. Write a short description of someone you know using at least three similes or metaphors.

B. Has someone entered your life and changed it, as Vida changed the author's life? Write about this person, and tell how he or she affected you.

C. What was *your* dream when you came to this country? Has it changed? If so, how?

UNIT 4 ◆ *Review*

◆◆◆◆◆◆◆◆◆◆◆◆◆◆◆◆◆◆◆◆◆◆◆◆◆◆◆◆◆◆◆◆◆

Texts	Main Characters
FAMILY PHOTOS	the young woman
THE MAN WHO CAME TO THE LAST FLOOR	the man from Puerto Rico
	the policeman
VIDA	Vida the author, Judith

Work individually, with a partner, or with a group to complete one of these tasks.

1. Each of the above characters went through a process of change. Were the results positive or negative (or somewhere in between)? Rank the characters on this scale. Explain your ranking.

   CHANGE
   positive
   results

   negative
   results

2. Compare any of the two characters above. Do they have similar or different reactions to changes in their lives?

3. Which character do you identify with most? Why?

Intersecting Cultures

Culture is the way of life that a group of people share: their customs, beliefs, values, and communication system. The stories in this unit depict events that occur when two cultures intersect, sometimes conflict and discomfort results, and we talk about "culture clash." In your journal, write about your experiences with "culture clash." What customs or behaviors in this country seem strange or make you feel uncomfortable?

111

Meet the Author

MARK MATHABANE *(born 1958)*

MARK MATHABANE grew up in desperate poverty in South Africa. He managed to overcome the hopelessness of the apartheid system in South Africa with a hard-won education, and in 1978 won a scholarship to an American university. In 1989, he published *Kaffir Boy in America*, from which the following passage is taken. In this memoir he tells what it is like to be black in the United States. Mr. Mathabane's writing is especially impressive given that English is his fifth language.

Mr. Mathabane lives with his American wife and two children in North Carolina.

1. Anticipate the Story

In this passage from *Kaffir Boy in America*, the black South African writer tells about his plans to marry Gail, a white American woman. He and Gail give the news to their families.

Find South Africa on the map on page 181. What do you think will happen when they break the news to their families? Individually or with a partner, write two questions you would like answered as you read.

_____

_____

_____

_____

_____

Before you read, look at the text. Note that it contains a lot of dialogue. In English, each time a new person speaks, a new paragraph begins. This helps the reader keep track of who is talking.

2. Global Reading

Read the story through as quickly as you can. Look for answers to the questions you have written.

Jot down your reactions or questions about the story here or in your journal. Share them with a partner or group.

reader response

HOW YOU READ

Is talking about what you read helpful? Can you use this strategy in the future in your schoolwork?

Kaffir Boy in America

◆◆

Mark Mathabane

GAIL AND I WANTED A QUIET WEDDING. During our two years together we had experienced the usual ups and downs of a couple learning to know, understand, and respect each other. But through it all we had forthrightly° confronted the weaknesses and strengths of each other's characters.

forthrightly: directly, honestly

2   Our racial and cultural differences enhanced° our relationship and taught us a great deal about tolerance, compromise, and open-mindedness. Gail sometimes wondered why I and other blacks were so preoccupied with° the racial issue, and I was surprised that she seemed oblivious° to the subtler° forms of racism in American society. We regularly compared our backgrounds. I would describe growing up in a large, close-knit family, my dealings with constant hunger and pain, my joy at finding nightly relief from the hard life in the ghetto in my mother's and Granny's stories, the only books I had, and my learning very early in life to take my destiny into my own hands. Gail would describe growing up, protected and loved, in a middle-class nuclear family in the suburbs of the Midwest, the abundance of toys at Christmas, the feasts at Thanksgiving, full meals each day, the security and pride of being an American.

enhanced: made better

preoccupied with: always thinking about

oblivious: forgetful, not thinking about

subtler: from *subtle*, hard to detect or see

3   Gail and I had no illusions° about what the future held for us as a married, mixed couple in America. The continual source of our strength was our mutual trust and respect.

illusions: unreal or false ideas or beliefs

4   We wanted to avoid the mistake made by many couples of marrying for the wrong reasons, and only finding out ten, twenty, or thirty years later that they were incompatible, that they hardly took the time to know each other, that they had glossed over° serious personality conflicts in the expectation that marriage would miraculously make everything work out right. That point was underscored by the fact that Gail's parents, after thirty-five years of marriage, were going through a bitter and painful divorce, which had devastated° Gail and for a time adversely affected our budding° relationship.

glossed over: minimized the importance of

devastated: deeply hurt

budding: developing

5   When Gail broached° the news of our wedding plans to her family she met with some resistance. Both her liberal-minded brothers, Paul, a research scientist at Cornell Medical School in Manhattan, and Dan, a psychologist in New York, advised her to wait a little longer before "taking such a big step." Even her mother, Deborah, who all along had been supportive° of our relationship, and even joked about when we were going to get married so she could have grandchildren, now counseled Gail to really be sure that she was doing the right thing.

broached: started talking about

supportive: approving, helpful

6   "So it was all right for me to date him, but it's wrong for me to marry him. Is his color the problem, Mom?" Gail later told me she asked her mother.

7   "No. Color has nothing to do with it. I must admit that at first I had my reservations° about a mixed marriage, prejudices you might even call them. But then I realized that as a mother I have to be supportive of whatever or whoever makes you happy. And when I met Mark I found him a charming and intelligent young man. Any mother would be proud to have him for a son-in-law. Yes, my friends talk. Some even express shock at what you're doing. But they live in a different world. So you see, Mark's color is not the problem. My biggest worry is that you may be marrying Mark for the same wrong reasons that I married your father. When we met I saw him as intelligent, charming, and caring. It was all so new, all so exciting, and we both thought, on the surface at least, that ours was an ideal marriage that would last forever. I realized only later that I didn't know your father very well when we married."

reservations: doubts, concerns

8   "But Mark and I have been together more than two years," Gail replied. "We've been through so much together. We've seen each other at our weakest many times. I'm sure that time will only confirm° what we feel deeply about each other."

confirm: to make firm or true, strengthen

9   "You may be right. But I still think that waiting won't hurt. You're only twenty-five."

10   "But his parents may be coming to the U.S., and wouldn't it be special if we were married during their visit?"

11   "It would be. Yet I still stick by my opinion. But remember it's your life. And anyone you choose to love I would love, too."

12   Gail's father, David, whom I had not yet met personally, approached our decision with a father-knows-best attitude. He basically asked the same questions as Gail's mother: Why the haste?° Who is this Mark? What's his immigration status? And when he learned of my problems with the immigration department, he immediately suspected that I was marrying his daughter in order to remain in the United States.

haste: hurry

13   "But Dad, that's unfair," Gail said.

14   "Then why the rush? Buy time,° buy time," he chanted.

buy time: delay, put off until later (colloquial)

15   "Mark has had problems with immigration before and has always taken care of them himself," Gail retorted. "In fact he made it very clear when we were discussing marriage that if I had any doubts about anything, I should not hesitate to cancel our plans."

16   "Well, that's what they all say. But I still believe everything is happening too fast. Your mother and I are going through hell because of a mistake we made which could have been easily avoided, if we had only waited a year, as we initially talked about doing. But then we changed our minds and decided not to wait that long. That was a mistake. I now think that had we waited, we might have found out things about each other then that would have revealed° that we were not meant for each other. I don't want my only daughter to make the same mistake. It would break my heart."

revealed: showed

17   "Dad, Mark and I love each other, even though we may get strange looks as we walk down the street," Gail said. "In society's eyes, we're not a perfect match. But at least I've learned to choose love over social acceptability."

18   Her father proceeded to quote statistics showing that mixed couples had higher divorce rates than same-race couples and gave examples of mixed couples he had counseled who were having marital difficulties.

19   "Have you thought about what your children would go through?" he asked.

20   "Dad, are you a racist?"°

21   "No, of course not. But you have to be realistic."

racist: person who believes his own race is superior

22   "Maybe our children will have some problems, but whose children don't? But one thing they'll always have: our love and devotion."

23   "That's idealistic. People can be very cruel toward biracial children."

24   "Dad, we'll worry about that when the time comes. If one had to resolve° all doubt before one acted, there would be very little done."

25   "Remember, it's never too late to change your mind."

26   Other relatives of Gail's voiced similar concerns, but I'm happy to say that none of them were overtly racist. Yes, there were one or two persons who, privately, were appalled° that a Daughter of the American Revolution would marry a black man. Gail's mother's mother, Susan Stork Scott, a descendant of Stephen Hopkins, who came to America on the *Mayflower,* had been active in the DAR, a national patriotic society founded in 1890.

27   In time everyone came to respect our decision.

28   On my part, I met with no resistance from my family. In fact my mother was delighted at the news and was quick to point out to me once again that under Botha's recent reforms, mixed couples were now legal, and that she had seen a few in Johannesburg.

29   "But Mama," I said, "Gail is as white as they come. Doesn't that bother you?"

30   "Why should I be bothered?" my mother asked. "She's a caring and intelligent human being, isn't she? I would be bothered if she drank and smoked and was lazy and disrespectful."

31   "But Mama," I went on. "What will people say?"

32   "Who cares what people say? Child, if I had cared what people said, given the many times they have poked their noses into my affairs, I would have done nothing in my life. I learned too late to care only about what my heart and conscience said, but learn I did. Life is too short to waste worrying about what people will say. They will always say what suits their fancy, and what satisfies their prejudices."

33   "Won't you have hang-ups° caring for light-skinned grandchildren?"

34   "I have been caring for white children all my life. A child is a child, whether black or white. It needs loving, hugging, and kissing." ◆

3. Focused Reading

In writing about his future marriage to Gail, the author mentions things that could help make his marriage successful and things to worry about. As you reread, put these words and phrases into groups. Add other ideas if you wish.

cultural differences	mutual trust and respect
Gail's mother's attitude	Gail's father's attitude
love	society's eyes
divorce statistics	biracial children
Mark's mother's attitude	

Things That Could Help Make the Marriage Successful	Things to Worry About

4. Analyze the Story

In groups, choose one of the following to discuss. Elect a group member to report your conclusions to the class.

A. Which one of the parents do you agree with most? Explain why.

B. What are the main differences between Mark and Gail? What are the main similarities? Are they a good match, in your opinion?

READING STRATEGY

In North American schools, students are expected to give personal opinions about what they read. Is this true in your country?

5. Look at Language

A. *This passage uses several word forms related to* **race** *(n.):* **racial** *(adj.),* **racism** *(n.),* **racist** *(n., adj.) and* **biracial** *(adj.).*

Complete these sentences. Look back to check your answers.

1–2. "Gail sometimes wondered why I and other blacks were so preoccupied with the ____racial____ issue, and I was surprised that she seemed oblivious to the subtler forms of _____ in American society." (paragraph 2)

3. "Dad, are you a _____ ?" (paragraph 20)

4. "People can be very cruel toward _____ children." (paragraph 23)

5. "Other relatives of Gail's voiced similar concerns, but I'm happy to say that none of them were overtly _____ ." (paragraph 26)

B. *The passage also uses several word forms related to* **marriage** *(n.):* **marry** *(v., past tense =* married*);* **get married** *(v., past tense =* got married*);* **married** *(adj.) and* **marital** *(adj.).*

Complete these sentences. Look back to check your answers.

1. "Gail and I had no illusions about what the future held for us as a _____, mixed couple in America." (paragraph 3)

2. " . . . Gail's parents, after thirty-five years of _____, were going through a bitter and painful divorce. . . ." (paragraph 4)

3. "Even [Gail's] mother, Deborah, who all along had been supportive of our relationship, and even joked about when we were going to get _____ so she could have grandchildren, now counseled Gail to really be sure that she was doing the right thing." (paragraph 5)

4. "'So it was all right for me to date him, but it's wrong for me to _____ him. Is color the problem, Mom?' Gail later told me she asked her mother." (paragraph 6)

5. "I realized only later that I didn't know your father very well when we _____ ." (paragraph 7)

6. "Her father . . . gave examples of mixed couples he had counseled who were having _____ difficulties." (paragraph 18)

6. Move Beyond the Story

Discussion

A. In your opinion, is it important to marry someone of the same religion? The same nationality? The same race? Why or why not?

B. Take a survey of some classmates. Ask: **What are the two most important qualities for a partner or spouse to have?** Write their responses on the chart.

Classmate's Name	The Two Most Important Qualities for a Partner	

sense of humor
open-mindedness
beauty
intelligence
wealth
kindness
seriousness
ambition
romance
sensitivity
cheerfulness
seriousness
playfulness

Discuss your results. Do your classmates have similar views about the ideal partner?

Writing

A. Have you ever witnessed or experienced racism? Write the story.

B. Write a reaction to the story. Tell your opinions or feelings about it.

Meet the Author

AMY TAN *(born 1952)*

AMY TAN was born in California, two and a half years after her parents immigrated to the United States from China. Ms. Tan visited China for the first time in 1987 and said, "As soon as my feet touched China, I became Chinese." In 1989, her first novel, *The Joy Luck Club*, was published to rave reviews. The following passage comes from this book.

Amy Tan lives in San Francisco with her husband.

1. Anticipate the Story

In the following excerpt from *The Joy Luck Club*, the narrator is
Waverly Jong, a Chinese-American woman in her thirties. She is
engaged to be married to Rich, who is Anglo-American. Waverly
arranges for Rich and her mother to meet for the first time. Waverly's
mother invites Rich to dinner, and Waverly wants her fiancé to make a
good impression on her hard-to-please mother. Unfortunately, Rich
makes many mistakes while eating in this Chinese home.

*Can you predict some of the problems he will have? Brainstorm
with the class.*

_____

_____

_____

_____

_____

> **READING STRATEGY**
>
> Making predictions
> before you read a text
> can help you focus
> better as you read.

2. Global Reading

*Read the story through as quickly as you
can. Did Rich make some of the mistakes
that you predicted? Which ones?*

*Jot down your reactions or questions about
the passage here or in your journal. Share
them with a partner or group.*

> **HOW YOU READ**
>
> Did you find the story
> funny? Why or why
> not? Discuss your
> reaction with the class.

> **reader response**

Four Directions

◆◆

Amy Tan

AFTER MUCH THOUGHT, I CAME UP WITH A BRILLIANT° PLAN. I concocted° a way for Rich to meet my mother and win her over.° In fact, I arranged it so my mother would want to cook a meal especially for him. I had some help from Auntie Suyuan. Auntie Su was my mother's friend from way back. They were very close, which meant they were ceaselessly tormenting° each other with boasts and secrets. And I gave Auntie Su a secret to boast° about.

2   After walking through North Beach one Sunday, I suggested to Rich that we stop by for a surprise visit to my Auntie Su and Uncle Canning. They lived on Leavenworth, just a few blocks west of my mother's apartment. It was late afternoon, just in time to catch Auntie Su preparing Sunday dinner.

3   "Stay! Stay!" she had insisted.

4   "No, no. It's just that we were walking by," I said.

5   "Already cooked enough for you. See? One soup, four dishes. You don't eat it, only have to throw it away. Wasted!"

6   How could we refuse? Three days later, Auntie Suyuan had a thank-you letter from Rich and me. "Rich said it was the best Chinese food he has ever tasted," I wrote.

7   And the next day, my mother called me, to invite me to a belated birthday dinner for my father. My brother Vincent was bringing his girlfriend, Lisa Lum. I could bring a friend, too.

8   I knew she would do this, because cooking was how my mother expressed her love, her pride, her power, her proof that she knew more than Auntie Su. "Just be sure to tell her later that her cooking was the best you ever tasted, that it was far better than Auntie Su's," I told Rich. "Believe me."

9   The night of the dinner, I sat in the kitchen watching her cook, waiting for the right moment to tell her about our marriage plans, that we had decided to get married next July, about seven months away. She was chopping eggplant into wedges, chattering at the same time about Auntie Suyuan: "She can only cook looking at a recipe. My instructions are in my fingers. I know what secret ingredients to put in just by using my nose!" And she was slicing° with such a ferocity,°

---

brilliant: very intelligent

concocted: planned

win her over: gain her favor or love

tormenting: teasing, annoying

boast: talk about something with too much pride

slicing: cutting

ferocity: fierceness, violence

seemingly inattentive to her sharp cleaver, that I was afraid her fingertips would become one of the ingredients of the red-cooked eggplant and shredded pork dish.

10   I was hoping she would say something first about Rich. I had seen her expression when she opened the door, her forced smile° as she scrutinized° him from head to toe, checking her appraisal° of him against that already given to her by Auntie Suyuan. I tried to anticipate what criticisms she would have.

11   Rich was not only *not* Chinese, he was a few years younger than I was. And unfortunately, he looked much younger with his curly red hair, smooth pale skin, and the splash of orange freckles across his nose. He was a bit on the short side, compactly built. In his dark business suits, he looked nice but easily forgettable, like somebody's nephew at a funeral. Which was why I didn't notice him the first year we worked together at the firm. But my mother noticed everything.

12   "So what do you think of Rich?" I finally asked, holding my breath.

13   She tossed the eggplant in the hot oil and it made a loud, angry hissing sound. "So many spots on his face," she said.

14   I could feel the pinpricks° on my back. "They're freckles. Freckles are good luck, you know," I said a bit too heatedly in trying to raise my voice above the din° of the kitchen.

15   "Oh?" she said innocently.

16   "Yes, the more spots the better. Everybody knows that."

17   She considered this a moment and then smiled and spoke in Chinese: "Maybe this is true. When you were young, you got the chicken pox. So many spots, you had to stay home for ten days. So lucky, you thought."

18   I couldn't save Rich in the kitchen. And I couldn't save him later at the dinner table.

19   He had brought a bottle of French wine, something he did not know my parents could not appreciate. My parents did not even own wineglasses. And then he also made the mistake of drinking not one but two frosted glasses full, while everybody else had a half-inch "just for taste."

20   When I offered Rich a fork, he insisted on using the slippery ivory chopsticks.° He held them splayed° like the knock-kneed legs of an ostrich° while picking up a large chunk of sauce-coated eggplant.

forced smile: unnatural smile

scrutinized: closely examined

appraisal: opinion

pinpricks: small holes made by a pin; her skin feels prickly

din: noise

chopsticks: two small sticks used by Asians to eat

splayed: spread out awkwardly

ostrich: a large bird with long legs, unable to fly

Halfway between his plate and his open mouth, the chunk fell on his crisp white shirt and then slid into his crotch.° It took several minutes to get Shoshana* to stop shrieking with laughter.

21   And then he had helped himself to big portions of the shrimp and snow peas, not realizing he should have taken only a polite spoonful, until everybody had had a morsel.°

22   He had declined° the sautéed new greens, the tender and expensive leaves of bean plants plucked before the sprouts turn into beans. And Shoshana refused to eat them also, pointing to Rich: "He didn't eat them! He didn't eat them!"

23   He thought he was being polite by refusing seconds, when he should have followed my father's example, who made a big show of taking small portions of seconds, thirds, and even fourths, always saying he could not resist another bite of something or other, and then groaning° that he was so full he thought he would burst.

24   But the worst was when Rich criticized my mother's cooking, and he didn't even know what he had done. As is the Chinese cook's custom, my mother always made disparaging remarks° about her own cooking. That night she chose to direct it toward her famous steamed pork and preserved vegetable dish, which she always served with special pride.

25   "Ai! This dish not salty enough, no flavor," she complained, after tasting a small bite. "It is too bad to eat."

26   This was our family's cue to eat some and proclaim it the best she had ever made. But before we could do so, Rich said, "You know, all it needs is a little soy sauce." And he proceeded to pour a riverful of the salty black stuff on the platter, right before my mother's horrified eyes.

27   And even though I was hoping throughout the dinner that my mother would somehow see Rich's kindness, his sense of humor and boyish charm, I knew he had failed miserably in her eyes.

28   Rich obviously had had a different opinion on how the evening had gone. When we got home that night, after we put Shoshana to bed, he said modestly, "Well. I think we hit it off *A-o-kay*."° ◆

crotch: the place where the legs join the body

morsel: small piece

declined: politely refused

groaning: making deep sounds of pain

made disparaging remarks: said bad things about

hit it off A-o-kay: got along very well (colloquial)

---

*Waverly's daughter.

3. Focused Reading

As you reread, underline some of the mistakes Rich made. When you finish reading, fill in the bubbles below with advice that Waverly could have given Rich before the dinner. Work with a partner if you wish.

4. Analyze the Story

In groups, choose one of the following to discuss. Elect a group member to report your conclusions to the class.

A. Do Rich and Waverly have the same view of what happened at dinner? What do you think they said to each other afterward? Have different people in your group role-play Rich and Waverly's discussion.

B. Why was the meeting unsuccessful? Who, if anyone, was responsible for the failure?

C. If you have Chinese classmates, prepare any questions you may have for them about this story.

5. Look at Language

Good writers use vivid language. They choose their words carefully to achieve the effect they want.

In the following paragraph from the story, eight vivid adjectives have been deleted. Read the passage without these important words.

> When I offered Rich a fork, he insisted on using the chopsticks. He held them splayed like the legs of an ostrich while picking up a chunk of eggplant. Halfway between his plate and his mouth, the chunk fell on his shirt and then slid into his crotch. It took several minutes to get Shoshana to stop shrieking with laughter.

Now read the original passage. How does the meaning change? In a small group, discuss why the author added these particular adjectives. What effect does each one have?

> When I offered Rich a fork, he insisted on using the **slippery ivory** chopsticks. He held them splayed like the **knock-kneed** legs of an ostrich while picking up a **large** chunk of **sauce-coated** eggplant. Halfway between his plate and his **open** mouth, the chunk fell on his **crisp white** shirt and then slid into his crotch. It took several minutes to get Shoshana to stop shrieking with laughter.

Try your hand at using vivid language. Insert one or more adjectives into each blank in the following passage. Read your passage to the class when you finish.

> John's eyes glanced over the _____ food on the _____ table. He picked up a _____ hot dog with his _____ hand and offered it to the _____ dog.

6. Move Beyond the Story

Discussion

A. Dinner customs vary widely around the world. According to what you've read in this story and observed elsewhere, what are some dinner customs in mainstream North America? How do they differ from dinner customs in your native countries?

B. Compare Rich and Waverly's future marriage with Mark and Gail's (from the last story, *Kaffir Boy in America*). Which marriage has a better chance of success, in your opinion? Why?

Writing

A. Write about a funny cross-cultural experience you have had.

B. Imagine that a North American friend is going to your country. Write a list of rules to help him or her get along well. When writing your rules, try to predict where the North American might make mistakes in your culture.

Challenge

Meet the Author

TAHIRA NAQVI *(born 1945)*

TAHIRA NAQVI was born and raised in Pakistan. She came to the United States to attend graduate school at Western Connecticut State University. Her short stories have appeared in many North American journals and anthologies. The following short story appears here for the first time.

Ms. Naqvi lives in Danbury, Connecticut, with her family, where she teaches English at Western Connecticut State University.

1. Anticipate the Story

In the following short story, "A Clean Break," the narrator is a teenage boy of Pakistani origin living in the United States. He tells about an incident a few years earlier that was very uncomfortable for him.

Read the first paragraph and the first sentence of the second paragraph. What do you think the story might be about? Write one or two predictions, and then discuss your ideas with the class.

READING STRATEGY

Good readers make predictions about the content of a text before and as they read.

_____

_____

_____

_____

_____

2. Global Reading

Read the story through for the general idea. Were you able to predict some of the content?

Jot down your reactions or questions about the story here or in your journal. Share them with a partner or group.

HOW YOU READ

Did predicting the story help your reading? What else helped you?

reader response

A Clean Break

◆◆◆◆◆◆◆◆◆◆◆◆◆◆◆◆◆◆◆◆◆◆◆◆◆◆◆◆◆◆◆◆◆◆◆

Tahira Naqvi

THING IS, I DON'T EAT PORK,° or ham, or for that matter, bacon. We aren't supposed to, you know, because the meat of the pig is *haram,* forbidden. That's one of the first things they tell you in Sunday Islamic class. Then they keep drumming it into your head° until the word *pork,* written or uttered, or in any other way implied, instantly conjures up° heinous° images.

pork: the flesh of a pig

drumming . . . head: repeating it many times

conjures up: brings to mind

heinous: terrible

2   Anyway, what I'm saying is that this is something that can lead to problems. Not severe ones, when one thinks of what's going wrong on a larger scale in the world, the ozone layer for example, and the fall of communism, but for a twelve-year-old whose life is confined within the restrictive limits of school and home, matters of ecology or political disintegration of a system thousands of miles away are entirely remote° and inconsequential.° The pork issue, on the other hand, is immediate, momentous, and disturbing. I can look back now and say all this with a certain degree of complacency° because I'm not twelve any more. My younger brother is. Sooner or later he'll find out the hard way that things are not always what they seem, and as I tell my story I know he must come to grips with° this knowledge alone, as I did.

remote: far away

inconsequential: unimportant

complacency: satisfaction

come to grips with: learn to accept

3   It was the summer of '82, or '83 perhaps. We didn't go to Pakistan that year, I got my first *A* in English, my first *D* in math, and that was also the year I mowed the lawn° for the very first time, taking three days to complete the job. Also that year Dan and I invested in our first copy of *Dirty Dames.* Actually my story unfolds at Dan's house on the occasion of *his* twelfth birthday, Dan to whom I confided my necessary aversion° to pork when we were in third grade and who responded by giving me a bite of his ham sandwich saying, with a completely straight face, "Want a bite of my sandwich? It's roast beef."

mowed the lawn: cut grass with a machine

aversion: strong dislike

I can't remember now why I was so eager to take a bite from his sandwich in the first place. I'll never forget how he roared and gurgled with laughter afterward.

4   Anyway, Dan's mother, Mrs. Gordon, was serving hot dogs, burgers, and ice cream, regular birthday fare. Now hot dogs are hot dogs. I mean you can't say no to one or people will tend to view you as weird.° Everyone eats hot dogs, even the strictest Muslims who won't eat any kind of meat except that which is *halal* or kosher.° So how was I going to put myself in a spot by asking Mrs. Gordon if the hot dogs sizzling° with such an air of detachment° on the grill were pork or beef?

5   You see, once a hot dog's been stripped of its wrapping and bared there's no way of telling just by looking at it if it's pork or anything else. Why not wait for the burgers? you might well ask. Well, simply because Mrs. Gordon was doing hot dogs first.

6   We'd been playing freeze-tag° for nearly an hour and were sweaty and hungry. The hot dogs, ready to perfection, their skins ruddy° and streaked with charcoal bands, looked, well, wonderful. My stomach growled audibly. Oh, what agony!

7   I must admit it had never been as bad as this. Ideas about escape presented themselves in a haphazard way as I followed Dan and the others in their trek toward food. I could take the hot dog and later toss it behind some bushes when no one was looking; I could take it and hide it under a pile of potato chips, eat the chips slowly, and *then* toss the hot dog behind some bushes; take the dreaded° thing into the house surreptitiously° and dispose of it in the kitchen trash and come out clean; politely decline the hot dog, saying, "I'm sick, I'm not supposed to eat any meat." The line before me diminished.° I still didn't know what I was going to do with the hot dog. All I knew was I going to take it and I wasn't going to eat it.

8   There was much hysteria° among us that afternoon. Mustard went flying on shirts and faces instead of being deposited neatly on the hot dogs, ketchup was squirted this way and that, some landing on our T-shirts, some in our hair. Dan was gurgling and roaring again. And on the grill, Mrs. Gordon's long, white, freckled arm poised over it with tongs, the hot dogs continued to hiss° maliciously.°

weird: strange

kosher: clean according to Jewish law

sizzling: cooking (with a hissing noise)

detachment: separation, lack of interest

freeze-tag: a children's game

ruddy: reddish

dreaded: feared, hated

surreptitiously: in a secret way

diminished: got smaller

hysteria: extreme excitement

hiss: make the sound of a snake

maliciously: harmfully

9   Uncertainty is a terrible thing. And it's never more disturbing than when one is among friends. I wiped my mouth with a paper napkin and heaped my plate high with chips. Soon the hot dog was buried under them. Where were the bushes? They were far, oh yes they were far, at the edge of the lawn, and beyond them was—the road! Frustration formed a knot in my stomach; I swore silently. There was nothing else to do except sneak into° the house and dump° the wretched° item.

sneak into: enter without being seen

dump: throw away

wretched: miserable, unhappy

10   I found myself in the kitchen. There wasn't anyone around. From the kitchen window I could see the whole gang devouring° their hot dogs. I could also see that Mrs. Gordon had put the hamburger patties on the grill and that they were already smoking. I looked around for a trash can. None was in sight. Sometimes they're hidden in the cabinet below the sink—why show the world your trash? I bent down.

devouring: eating hungrily

11   "Is that you Hada?"

12   Startled,° I straightened up quickly to find myself face to face with Dan's grandmother, whom all of us called Mrs. G.

startled: surprised

13   "Hi Mrs. G."

14   "How are you this afternoon? Enjoying your hot dog, I see."

15   If she only knew. "Yeah," I lied. We chatted for a moment longer while she rummaged through a cabinet. What was she looking for?

16   "See you later, Mrs. G.," I said, and made a swift exit through the kitchen door while her back was turned to me.

17   It would have been foolish to join my friends with the uneaten hot dog still in my plate. Nobody takes this long to eat one lousy° hot dog. Frantically I looked around, wondering what my next move should be. My hand was numb,° the fingers curled around the limp and soggy paper plate stiff. And I was awfully, dreadfully hungry. My insides convulsed° and my stomach growled fiercely. On the other side of the lawn, where the woods began, Dan and the others were beginning a game of tag. Dan gesticulated. "Come on," he said, "we're waiting."

lousy: small, insignificant

numb: without feeling

my insides convulsed: my internal organs moved violently

18   I decided to return to the kitchen. Perhaps Mrs. G. had found what she was looking for and was gone. I peered through the kitchen door. No sign of her. I darted in, deposited the weary° hot dog along

weary: tired

with the bent, enfeebled° plate on the kitchen counter and turned to leave. Something held me back. I looked around. What was it?

19   Mrs. Gordon's counters were bare° and uncluttered, unlike my mother's which had a toaster, toaster oven, food processor, blender, everything, out . . . . permanently. Where did Dan's mother hide her appliances? Anyway, this is what it was. Sitting on the clean, spotless counter, the plate with the hot dog and a few solitary chips clinging dejectedly° to one side of the hot dog stood out as if it were on display. Like an Andy Warhol painting. The napkin was ragged and congealed with a combination of mustard and ketchup.

20   Hastily I swooped up° the plate again and made for° the trash can that I knew was in the cabinet under the kitchen sink.

21   "Hey man, what's up? You coming?" Dan had come looking for me.

22   "Yeah," I said, letting go of the plate in my hand. It fell soundlessly into the darkness of the trash can. I sighed in relief.

23   Later, after I had consumed, with unnatural urgency, two burgers and more fries, we helped Mrs. Gordon clean up. As we picked up cartons to take back into the house my eyes fell on some hot dogs still intact in their wrappings. Beef, beef, beef, was all I saw.

24   But like I said, once a hot dog has been stripped and bared, there's no way of telling if it's beef or anything else. ◆

enfeebled: weak

bare: empty

dejectedly: sadly

swooped up: grabbed quickly

made for: went toward (colloquial)

3. Focused Reading

Reread the story. Fill in the blanks in the summary below.

This story is about a _____ boy, Hada, who, for

religious reasons, cannot _____ . At a birthday party

for _____ , grilled _____ are served. Hada

does not know if they are pork or _____ . He is

afraid to ask. He accepts one because he doesn't want to

look _____ . But once the horrible thing is on his

plate, he knows he must _____ . He considers

throwing it in the bushes, but they are _____ . He

sneaks into the _____ looking for a trash can, but

Dan's grandmother catches him there. Hot dog in hand, he

returns outside, where Dan calls him to come and play. He

escapes back into the kitchen. Just as he is reaching under the

sink, Dan _____ , but he succeeds in dumping it

without Dan seeing. In the end, Hada discovers that all of his

fears were for nothing. The hot dogs were made

of _____ !

4. Analyze the Story

*In groups, choose one of the following to discuss. Elect a group
member to report your conclusions to the class.*

A. Imagine that Hada had simply refused the hot dog. What would
    have happened? How would the story change? Were Hada's
    fears realistic?

B. The author tells this story from the point of view of a teenage
    boy, who narrates the story. What words, phrases, and
    expressions does the narrator use that emphasize his youth?
    Underline them in the story.

5. Look at Language

Adverbs give more information about a verb; they tell **how** something is done. Adverbs can often be formed by adding **-ly** to adjectives.

The following adverbs are used in the story to add emphasis to verbs. Fill in the sentences below with adverbs from the list, and then look back at the text to see if the author's choices match yours.

Adverbs	Formed from	Adjectives
quickly		quick
silently		silent
frantically		frantic
hastily		hasty
soundlessly		soundless
fiercely		fierce
dejectedly		dejected
maliciously		malicious

1. "And on the grill, Mrs. Gordon's long, white, freckled arm poised over it with tongs, the hot dogs continued to hiss _____." (paragraph 8)

2. "Frustration formed a knot in my stomach; I swore _____." (paragraph 9)

3. "Startled, I straightened up _____ to find myself face to face with Dan's grandmother. . . . " (paragraph 12)

4. "It would have been foolish to join my friends with the uneaten hot dog still in my plate. Nobody takes this long to eat one lousy hot dog. _____ I looked around, wondering what my next move should be." (paragraph 17)

5. "My insides convulsed and my stomach growled _____." (paragraph 17)

6. "Sitting on the clean, spotless counter, the plate with the hot dog and a few solitary chips clinging _____ to one side of the hot dog stood out as if it were on display. Like an Andy Warhol painting." (paragraph 19)

7. "_____ I swooped up the plate again and made for the trash can that I knew was in the cabinet under the kitchen sink." (paragraph 20)

8. "[The plate] fell _____ into the darkness of the trash can. I sighed in relief." (paragraph 22)

6. Move Beyond the Story

Discussion

A. How does food or drink in your country differ from here? Are similar things eaten for breakfast, lunch, and dinner?

B. In a group with students from one or two other countries, discuss eating customs. In your countries, is it appropriate to do the following things when you are an invited dinner guest? Is it in this country? At the top of the following chart write your country's name (col 1), your classmate's (col 2, 3), this country's name (col 4). Go through the list of eating customs and write ok or no for each country.

1. eat quickly				
2. talk a lot				
3. put elbows on table				
4. eat with the fingers				
5. ask for seconds				
6. refuse food				
7. make eating noises				
8. leave food on plate				
9. use a toothpick				
10. pick up bread with the left hand				

Writing

A. Think back to your adolescent or teenage years. Do you remember an event that was traumatic, embarrassing, or difficult? Write the story.

B. Was there ever a time in your life when you felt, like Hada, very uncomfortable because you did not fit in? Write the story.

Challenge

Meet the Author

NAHID RACHLIN

NAHID RACHLIN was born and raised in Iran. She has written two highly acclaimed novels about living between two cultures, *Foreigner* and *Married to a Stranger*. The story that appears here also deals with the problems of crossing cultures. It was first published in *Redbook* magazine in 1988.

Ms. Rachlin lives with her American-born husband in New York City, where she teaches creative writing at Barnard College.

1. Anticipate the Story

The following story is about an old Greek man, Alexander, who travels to the United States to see his son, Gregory, a doctor. They haven't seen each other for eight years.

Find Greece on the map on page 181. Then read the title and the first two paragraphs of the story. What do you think will happen? Write some questions that you would like answered as you read the rest of the story.

READING STRATEGY

Many texts give important general information in the first few paragraphs. It is a good idea to read these first and then stop to ask yourself questions about what will follow.

_____

_____

_____

_____

2. Global Reading

Read the rest of the story through as quickly as you can. Try to find answers to the questions you have written.

Jot down your reactions or questions about the story here or in your journal. Share them with a partner or group.

reader response

Journey of Love

◆◆◆

Nahid Rachlin

BEFORE HE LEFT FOR THE VISIT, Alexander Litsios had a suit made for himself by the best tailor in Argos, then bought a few ties and a pair of shoes. He had not seen Gregory for eight years. At the beginning, when Gregory first went to the United States, he had come home for visits a few times but then, once he was finished with his studies in medical school, he stopped coming. It was hard for him to take off,° he said, while he was trying to build up a practice. When he got married, he wanted to bring his wife over but one thing led to another and they never managed the trip.

take off: take a vacation

2   On the airplane Alexander stared out the window at the clouds, one moment a sea of gold and the next, foam. His mind kept drifting to Gregory. He had been a lively, curious boy, a sensitive and introspective adolescent° and, when a little older, before he left, a sociable, ambitious, and good-natured young man. Now he was married to an American woman and he had set up a house and practice° on Long Island. Perhaps he had changed a great deal. Alexander's heart beat with the anticipation of seeing him after all these years.

adolescent: teenager

practice: business; in this case, a medical office

3   At Kennedy Airport, going through the customs line, Alexander was apprehensive.° The customs officers, tall cold-looking men, searched his suitcases and the inside of his violin case—he had brought his violin because he liked playing it every day. They opened up the tin box in which he had packed the goat cheese Margarita made. One of the men said something to the other, which Alexander could not understand, and then put the box away on the other side of the counter. But they let him take everything else. As he entered the vast hall beyond the customs line, he looked for Gregory but could not spot him. Panic came over him. At his age of eighty, it was hard to travel so far and he knew very little English. He saw people everywhere, people hurrying, people on phones. . . . He looked this way and that, growing dizzy° with the chaos.°

apprehensive: uneasy, fearful

dizzy: unsteady, confused

chaos: confusion, disorder

4   Suddenly a man was coming toward him, smiling. "Father," he called.

5   "Gregory, my son."

6   Gregory had gained weight and his movements were heavy, Alexander noticed.

7   The two of them embraced quickly and kissed.

8   "You look very well," Alexander said, though inwardly he shrank a bit from° Gregory's unfamiliar image.

shrank . . . from: turned away from

9   "You look well too," Gregory said excitedly, his voice trembling a little. "It has been so long. . . . I can't believe you're really here. . . ." He moved closer to his father and they embraced again, first hesitantly and then more firmly.

10   "Susan is waiting in the car," Gregory then said, pulling back. "It was hard to park around here. You have to tell me all about Mother and Carolyn. . . . Susan and I have been looking forward to your coming."

11   Outside, Susan was standing by the car, a dark blue Mercedes. She and Alexander greeted each other and kissed. She was tall, thin. In the dim light he could see that she was blond. She smiled at him and said something to him in English that he assumed was an expression of welcome. He smiled back and nodded a few times as he got into the back seat.

12   They drove along vast highways and then through a string of small towns. "That's our house," Gregory eventually said, pointing to a white shingled house set alongside similar homes on a wide, tree-lined street. The street and the houses had an oddly empty and quiet feeling to them, as if they were deserted.°

deserted: abandoned, left suddenly

13   When they got inside, Gregory said, "Let me take you to the room we set up for you. It's the lightest room in the house. I thought you'd like all the sunlight pouring in during the day."

14   "You shouldn't have gone to any trouble," Alexander said.

15   "Please, make yourself comfortable," Susan said half in English and half in Greek. "Make this your home."

16   Gregory carried Alexander's suitcases into the room. Alexander carried the violin.

17   "I'm glad you brought your violin," Gregory said.

18   "You used to like me to play it for you," Alexander said, smiling. He began to pull a few things from one of the suitcases—his bathrobe, a pair of slippers.

19   "There's a bathroom right there if you feel like taking a shower," Gregory said. "Take your time. We'll be waiting for you in the living room."

20 After Gregory left, Alexander went into the bathroom. His muscles were aching from the plane ride and he stood under the shower for a long time. Margarita must be with Carolyn right now, helping her with the children, he thought, feeling sad that they had not come along on the trip. Carolyn, the daughter, had just had a baby and her other two children were very young. He had been away from them only for a day but it seemed much longer. . . .

21 The hard drops of warm water on his skin at last had a soothing effect. But as he stepped out of the shower, he was startled°—the floor was covered with water, some of it leaking out into the hallway. He realized he should have put the curtain inside of the tub before he turned on the water. At home, their large deep bath had a door on it and the shower was set far in the back of the tub. He stood for a moment, frozen by embarrassment. Finally, he called Gregory.

startled: surprised

22 Gregory came in promptly.°

promptly: immediately

23 "Look what I've done," Alexander said.

24 Gregory stared at the floor, then at his father. His heart gave a squeeze° at the shame° registered on his father's face. "Don't worry about it. It's nothing—it happens all the time. I'll mop it up."

squeeze: a firm pressure

shame: a painful feeling of guilt or dishonor

25 "I'm an old man, I don't know what I'm doing," Alexander said apologetically.

26 A few moments later Alexander saw Gregory, through the half-open door of the guest room, standing in the hallway and whispering something to Susan—maybe about the flooding.° His heart sank lower and lower. . . .

flooding: overflowing of water

27 In half an hour the three of them were sitting in the living room talking. They talked about Carolyn and Margarita, reminisced° about other relatives and friends Gregory had left behind. One of his high school friends was now in Athens, working for the Ministry of Education, and another owned a vineyard, Alexander told him.

reminisced: remembered past events

28 Gregory and Susan's living room was furnished in a modern, functional style. The rug Alexander had brought over as a present, now spread on a couch, stood out vividly° because of its bright colors. He had shopped for the rug himself, going from store to store until he had found one in a fine pink and maroon weave. He had also brought two

stood out vividly: was very noticeable

sweaters that Margarita had knitted, one for Gregory and one for Susan, green and blue for him and yellow and blue for her, and some silver jewelry for her. They all lay on the table, looking alien° in that room.

alien: foreign, strange

29   "I must get to bed now," Gregory said after they had had a few drinks. "I have to see patients early in the morning. But I've scheduled a few days off at the beginning of November to take you around to see more of the country."

30   They all got up. Alexander went to bed immediately but he had a hard time sleeping. The bedroom was furnished in dark teak,° a contrast to the stark white walls. The blanket on the bed was a khaki color, the kind he had seen in hospitals. In fact, the room, and what he had seen of the house, had an antiseptic° look he associated with institutions. The silence was oppressive. Except for an occasional car passing by, there was no hint of human life. His mind filled with worries. Was the baby going to be all right? (He had been a month premature° and was delicate for his age.) Did Margarita remember to take the sick goat to the veterinarian? Would the young boy who came to take care of the olive and fruit trees in their yard be neglectful° now with Alexander away? He covered his head with the blanket and curled up his body; and in that position he finally fell asleep.

teak: the wood of a large East Indian tree

antiseptic: free from microorganisms or infection

premature: too early

neglectful: careless

31   Gregory lay in bed next to Susan, anxious about his father. He had seemed out of his element in the house, like a lost child. It would have been better if he and Susan had gone to Argos instead, Gregory thought. There, the visit would not be so focused and concentrated. His mother, sister, and relatives would be around to absorb them. Yet he had wanted his father to see something of his life. He had wanted to make his family proud by becoming a doctor, a doctor trained in the United States. It had required so many years, so much work and concentration, that it was hard for him to remember who he used to be; the changes that had come over him had been so gradual.° For instance, falling in love with Susan and marrying her had been natural at the time, but his marriage was part of losing his old self.

gradual: happening slowly

32   The next day, when Alexander awoke, Gregory had already left for his office. Susan served him breakfast at the kitchen counter and the two of them made attempts° to talk, using what they knew of the

made attempts: tried

other's language. After breakfast she drove him around Setauket, passing a post office, a bank, a supermarket, a pond with white ducks floating on its surface, and then to some of the surrounding towns.

33   At lunchtime they went to Gregory's office, in Setauket also, not far from the house. It was shiny with modern equipment. Gregory introduced him to two young women, a nurse and a secretary. They greeted Alexander with smiles. Then he, Gregory, and Susan went out to eat at a fish restaurant overlooking the Long Island Sound.

34   "I have a little extra time," Gregory said to him. "A patient cancelled. Maybe you would like to get some clothes."

35   Alexander was puzzled. "I don't need any clothes," he said. "I brought enough with me."

36   "It won't hurt to have some more, Dad. Your suit is a little old-fashioned now." Gregory smiled.

37   So they went to a department store in the mall and managed to find a suit and shirts in his size, though he was shorter and more broadly built than most American men.

38   "Do you want to get a haircut too?" Gregory asked.

39   Alexander shrugged. His hair, still reasonably full, was long at the edges, a little disheveled.° "Why not?"

disheveled: untidy, messy

40   There was a salon right next to the department store. Inside, men and women were sitting on plush swivel chairs, their hair being cut. Gregory talked to a man behind a desk. Something was said on a loudspeaker and a young woman came over to lead Alexander to the washing area. Gregory said he had to go back to work but Susan would wait for him. Alexander's hair was washed and then cut by another young woman in less than an hour. At home he went to the local barber, where sometimes it took a whole afternoon to have his hair cut—they gossiped about town events and drank tea.

41   After the haircut Susan took Alexander home, then left to go to work; she had a parttime job as an interior decorator. Alexander wandered through the empty, unfamiliar house, leafing through magazines and newspapers, listening to music. When Gregory returned home in the evening, he looked exhausted.° He hardly talked to him or to Susan. He retired to bed even earlier than the night before. Susan watched television and Alexander sat on the sofa, dispirited,° his hands folded on his lap.

exhausted: very tired

dispirited: depressed, sad

42   A week had gone by . . . slowly. Gregory was usually gone by the time Alexander awoke. Alexander had breakfast with Susan and then she went about doing the household chores. After she was done with that, she usually did a little gardening, pulling weeds out of the flower beds or turning the water hose on the grass. Once, looking on the refrigerator door, Alexander found a note, held by a magnet, that Susan had left for Gregory. He could read a few of the words: "Try not to be too late tonight." Underneath the note, Gregory had written: "I'll try but you know I can't help it sometimes." The next day he found another note, with Susan saying, "I love you," and Gregory writing back, "I love you, too. Be patient." Be patient with what? Anyway, it was odd that they would leave notes to each other. Was their time so precious— or was it hard for them to say certain things to each other? He recalled how shy Gregory had been with women, rarely seeking them out for pleasure as he himself had when he was young, before he got married. Still, Susan seemed difficult to talk to. There was something abrupt° and awkward° about her. He might not have been comfortable talking with her even if he knew the language better. She was very different from Margarita and Carolyn, with their soft, fleshy bodies, the ease of their movements. Thinking of them, and of home, Alexander tried to pass time by practicing English, using a book Gregory had given to him, or taking walks in the neighborhood, though it was not that pleasant with no sidewalks anywhere and nothing except houses to look at. He thought of playing the violin but he had no desire to.

abrupt: sudden and short in behavior or speech

awkward: clumsy, uncomfortable

43   Gregory rarely came home for lunch—he said he had to be at the hospital to check on patients. Too bad, Alexander thought, lunch was such a joyful event at home. Relatives and friends got together and spent a long time on the meal—five, six courses. They caught up with the events of each other's lives. No matter what problems might weigh on their chests, they would feel lifted after sharing them with others. Annoyances,° grudges° a person might bear another person, would be at least temporarily forgotten. Alexander was tempted° to take Gregory aside and talk to him about all this, the way he used to: Gregory would lie on the sofa and he would sit at its edge, leaning over him a little, and they would talk late into the night. . . .

annoyances: things that bother or disturb

grudges: bad feelings against someone

was tempted: wanted

44   The days began to blend together. Susan would feed Alexander a light lunch, a sandwich, soup from a can, and then drop him off at the mall before she went to work. He wandered around by himself. He looked into store windows or sat on a bench and watched the shoppers. He wore his own clothes instead of the ones Gregory bought for him. He liked their familiarity but he was now conscious that they made him seem a little out of place, neglectful of his appearance. He sometimes bought fruit from a supermarket, though the cellophane wrapped around it made it look artificial. The market was very different from the one at home, where heaps° of fruits and vegetables were displayed on carts and you could touch and pick the ones you wanted. Here, everything was hidden behind something, wrapped up in paper, set behind glass. He was aware of a gulf° between himself and the world around him. Every minute crawled, slowly, slowly. "This is like prison," he said aloud once. No one seemed to have heard him. Everyone went by indifferently.° Their faces were so dispassionate° that a substance other than blood could be running in their veins. There was no public transportation, there were no cabs° to hail, so he had to stay in the mall for four hours until Susan was finished with work and picked him up.

heaps: big piles

gulf: a wide gap or separation

indifferently: not caring

dispassionate: calm, not passionate

cabs: taxicabs

45   What was he going to tell Margarita and Carolyn when he returned home? If he had to describe what he had seen of this country, he would say that it existed in twilight,° dim and gray. The trip was supposed to be for three months but Alexander was already doubting that he could last that long. Gregory must have given up° a lot of himself to adjust to this world. There was something like denial that went with his attitude. It was as if he were trying hard to conceal° a feeling from everyone, maybe unhappiness, a shame of some kind? It was hard to know what went on in his heart and mind—whatever he truly felt seemed deeply buried, unreachable to Alexander, and maybe even to himself. Gregory, the one he knew from the past, simply was not there. Gregory—the child, the adolescent, the young adult—was barely represented in this man. Still, the love Alexander felt for him remained, an entity unto itself, inside his heart.

twilight: time of day between sunset and darkness

given up: sacrificed

conceal: hide

46   Growing up, Gregory had imagined a greater happiness for himself than the one he could find in his hometown. And Alexander, caught in Gregory's dream, worked hard and lived for that distant, misty future. Alexander had been a carpenter, going from house to house, building cabinets, restoring° old wooden walls or floors. His job had satisfied him, when he could do it in a leisurely manner. It gave

restoring: fixing

him the chance to build things out of pieces of wood and enjoy their completion into shapes, and at the same time left his mind free to contemplate.° As Gregory grew older, Alexander had had to work harder, taking on unpleasant jobs in factories or at building sites. He had hoped Gregory would return home, set up an office and buy a house, maybe on a hill. But this had turned out to be° that future, a world that did not include him. . . .

contemplate: think

turned out to be: became

47   As Gregory drove home from his office on a late afternoon, he thought: My poor father, he must be terribly bored, having to spend so much time alone. I must try harder to get home earlier, make attempts to talk to him more. He constantly seems on the verge° of wanting to say something to me. But how can he and I have a satisfactory talk? How can I sum up° for him what I cannot for myself?

on the verge: on the edge

sum up: summarize

48   He remembered Susan had left a note for him to get some butter and milk. He parked his car by the supermarket and went in. By the produce counter he noticed bags of dried fruit. His father, and he himself, liked dried cherries. He picked up a couple of bags and put them in the cart.

49   At home he found his father sitting on the living room sofa while Susan was preparing dinner in the kitchen. After he kissed Susan and unloaded the groceries, he went over to his father and handed him the bags of cherries. "These are for you, Dad."

50   "Dried cherries," Alexander said, a faint smile coming over his face. He opened the bag and took a few cherries out, giving some to Gregory.

51   Gregory sat next to his father. "Not as good as the ones at home," he said after eating one. "Remember we used to pick cherries from the orchard? Mother dried them out in the sun."

52   "Yes," his father said wistfully.

53   "I wish Mother had been able to come along with you." But, as he said that, Gregory was aware of a pressure on his chest. Having his mother in the house with Susan would have been so difficult. She might have tried to instruct Susan in cooking or walked around the house frowning° at the decor.° As he imagined this, he could sense how formal and stiff° the house truly was. He started to say something about it to his father but it was very hard. He was aware of a pool of tension° collecting in the air between them.

frowning: expressing disapproval

decor: the way a house is decorated or arranged

stiff: not relaxed

tension: mental or nervous strain

54   "I'd better help Susan set the table," he said, getting up. "We'll be eating soon," he added in a voice that he tried to make robust.°

robust: full of energy

55   One night after Alexander had been visiting for three weeks, he lay in bed thinking he was an unwanted guest with no one to talk to. He got out of bed and looked at the street. It was completely empty. The lights above the house doors shone, but for what? Not even a car went by. In Argos you could see people at all hours of the night. A woman still awake would look out of a window, a group of restless teenagers would be standing under the streetlights, men singly or together would be returning home from a bar or a coffee shop. A loud argument between a husband and wife or a son and father would rumble out of a house. Music would be playing somewhere.

56   He listened to see if there were any signs of awakening from Gregory and Susan's room but the second floor, where they slept, was dark and silent. He paced the room for a moment, back and forth, and in circles. Then, impulsively,° he put his long woolen poncho around him and went into the yard, carrying his violin. He suddenly had a strong desire to play it, to penetrate° the silence. He sat under a maple tree, above which the moon dangled, and he began to play. He played melodies from his childhood. The strings were already out of tune from lack of use and he could not tighten them just right, but the sound they made gave him pleasure anyway; he had missed it so much. He played softly, using the low scale. Shadows of the trees and the houses cast definite, vivid shapes across the lawn. Every leaf, every flower, was sharply delineated.° He could almost hear Gregory's voice as a child, saying to him, "Play more." He began to play louder and louder, using sharper notes.

impulsively: without thinking

penetrate: make a way into something

delineated: drawn

57   He saw several windows opening on the houses across the street. He saw heads leaning out of them and pulling back. His heart began to beat with excitement. The melody enveloped° him. He was locked inside of it, lifted into another arena, he was not sure for how long. . . .

enveloped: surrounded

58   Gregory was saying, "Father, what's going on? A neighbor just threatened to call the police."

59   Confusion surrounded Alexander like fog. Gregory seemed like a figure from a bad dream, leaning out of the window, his face glowing with an eerie° light, and talking with an abrupt, jerking motion of his hands. Susan came and stood next to Gregory, looking on silently.

60   Alexander went on playing, though he had begun to shiver.° His teeth were chattering.

61   "Father . . ." Gregory was now walking rapidly toward him. "Come inside, Father, it's the middle of the night."

62   "I want to go back home, to our own warm sun," Alexander said. "I'm cold, I'm always shivering."

63   Gregory and Susan tried to talk Alexander into staying a while longer. But he wanted to leave as soon as possible. He was not feeling well, he said; he wanted to be in his own familiar surroundings.

64   After he saw his father off at the airport, on the way home Gregory burst out crying. He had not done that for a long time, not since he was refused by several medical schools. He could not get over the nagging guilt he felt that the visit had been a failure. What could he have done to improve it? He did not know. Susan must have had similar feelings. "I wasn't a good enough hostess," she had told him ruefully.

65   He thought of his father on the plane, over the Atlantic, a small old man barely filling the seat. He had no importance in the world; he would be invisible except for the love of his family and fellow villagers. Gregory tried to conjure up° memories of his childhood, the long walks in fragrant cherry orchards, hand in hand with his father. But the happy, peaceful thoughts would not come. Instead, he felt a pain unlike any he had every known. Now he longed° to hear his father's violin music once again—even in the dead of the night, even above the shouts of angry neighbors. Gregory had left something behind in Greece, something once tangible° and alive but no longer within his reach. ◆

eerie: strange, frightening

shiver: shake, as from cold or fear

conjure up: make appear as if by magic

longed: wanted very much

tangible: that can be touched

3. Focused Reading

Alexander, from a small town in Greece, experiences culture clash in suburban America. As you reread the story, note which specific differences he encounters. Put a check (√) in the right-hand column next to any of Alexander's North American experiences that match your own.

READING STRATEGY

When a text compares two things, making a chart will help you read and remember.

Argos, Greece	suburban USA	
the streets are busy, full	the streets are deserted	

Compare your notes with a classmate and talk about your own experiences of culture clash.

If you have Greek classmates, prepare any questions you have for them.

HOW YOU READ

Did you find information in this text that matches your own experience of North America? Remember: Good readers link what they know to what they read.

4. Analyze the Story

In groups, choose one of the following to discuss. Elect a group member to report your conclusions to the class.

A. "(Gregory) could not get over the nagging guilt he felt that the visit had been a failure. What could he have done to improve it? He did not know." Discuss this quotation. Was the visit a total failure, in your opinion? What could Gregory have done to improve it?

B. Discuss the scene where Alexander goes outside to play his violin. Where in the story does the scene occur? Why did the writer put it there?

C. Think about the future of the characters in the story. What will happen to them?

5. Look at Language

A symbol is something—usually a concrete image—that represents something else or has a larger meaning. A symbol often represents something abstract, as when a dove represents peace or a cross represents Christianity.

In this story, some things can be seen as symbols having a larger meaning. Can you attach meanings to any of the following? Work with a group.

Symbol	Possible Meaning
the gifts Alexander brings	They look "alien." Maybe they represent his feeling of not fitting in.
the violin	
the dried cherries Alexander buys	
the decor of Gregory's house	
the notes Gregory and Susan leave each other	

6. Move Beyond the Story

Discussion

A. Alexander didn't like much of what he saw in the United States.

> If he had to describe what he had seen of this country, he would say that it existed in twilight, dim and gray.

Take a survey of some of your classmates. Find out how they would describe life in North America to someone back in their country.

B. In a small group, prepare a role-play of the following scene: Alexander arrives home and greets his wife and daughter. What do they say? What does he say?

Writing

A. Gregory changed. He "had left something behind in Greece." What about you? Have you left part of yourself behind?

B. Write your reactions to the story and to Gregory and Alexander's feelings. Do you identify with either of these characters? If so, how? If not, why not?

UNIT 5 ◆ *Review*

◆◆

Texts	Main Characters
KAFFIR BOY IN AMERICA	Mark Gail Gail's mother Gail's father Mark's mother
FOUR DIRECTIONS	Waverly Rich Waverly's mother
A CLEAN BREAK	Hada Dan
JOURNEY OF LOVE	Gregory Susan Alexander (Gregory's father)

Work individually, with a partner, or with a group to complete one of these tasks.

1. Which character is, in your opinion,

   a. the most interesting? _____

   b. the most likeable? _____

   c. the least likeable? _____

   d. the most open and tolerant? _____

   e. the most like you? _____

   Support your opinions.

2. Take a class survey. Ask: **Which text did you like best? Why?** Post your results on a bulletin board.

3. Compare the situations in which Mark, Rich, Hada, and Alexander find themselves. Are there any similarities? Which character is in the most difficult situation, in your opinion?

UNIT 6

Facing Discrimination

The stories in this unit are about discrimination and cruelty experienced by members of minority groups within North America. In your journal, write about your experience in North America (or elsewhere). Have you ever felt or seen prejudice, injustice, or cruelty of one group against another?

Meet the Author

RICHARD RODRIGUEZ *(born 1944)*

RICHARD RODRIGUEZ, the son of Mexican immigrants, began his schooling in California, knowing just fifty words of English. He went on to study at Columbia University in New York. Mr. Rodriguez earns his living as a writer. He has published two books as well as numerous articles in newspapers and national magazines. The following excerpt is taken from his highly praised autobiography, *Hunger of Memory: The Education of Richard Rodriguez* (1982). The book tells of his struggles growing up in two cultures and with two languages.

Mr. Rodriguez lives in San Francisco, California.

1. Anticipate the Story

The following text from the autobiography *Hunger of Memory* is the first part of a chapter called "Complexion." (*Complexion* is the color and texture of one's skin.) In this text, the author remembers his childhood in California in the 1950s.

Read the first two paragraphs. What do you think the text will be about? Write one or two predictions, and then discuss your ideas with the class.

READING STRATEGY

Good readers make predictions about the content of a text before and as they read.

_____

_____

_____

_____

2. Global Reading

Read the story through for the general idea. Were you able to predict some of the content?

Jot down your reactions or questions about the story here or in your journal. Then share them with a partner or group.

reader response

Complexion

◆•

Richard Rodriguez

VISITING THE EAST COAST or the gray capitals of Europe during the long months of winter, I often meet people at deluxe hotels who comment on my complexion. (In such hotels it appears nowadays a mark of leisure°and wealth° to have a complexion like mine.) Have I been skiing? In the Swiss Alps? Have I just returned from a Caribbean vacation? No. I say no softly but in a firm voice that intends to explain: My complexion is dark. (My skin is brown. More exactly, terra-cotta° in sunlight, tawny° in shade. I do not redden in sunlight. Instead, my skin becomes progressively dark; the sun singes° the flesh.)

2   When I was a boy the white summer sun of Sacramento would darken me so, my T-shirt would seem bleached against my slender dark arms. My mother would see me come up the front steps. She'd wait for the screen door to slam° at my back. "You look like a *negrito*,"* she'd say, angry, sorry to be angry, frustrated almost to laughing, scorn.° "You know how important looks° are in this country. With *los gringos*† looks are all that they judge on. But you! Look at you! You're so careless!" Then she'd start in all over again. "You won't be satisfied till you end up looking like *los pobres* who work in the fields, *los braceros*."

3   (*Los braceros:* Those men who work with their *brazos*, their arms; Mexican nationals who were licensed to work for American farmers in the 1950s. They worked very hard for very little money, my father would tell me. And what money they earned they sent back to Mexico to support their families, my mother would add. *Los pobres*—the poor, the pitiful, the powerless ones. But paradoxically° also powerful men. They were the men with brown-muscled arms I stared at in awe° on Saturday mornings when they showed up downtown like gypsies to shop at Woolworth's or Penney's. On Monday nights they would gather hours early on the steps of the Memorial Auditorium for the wrestling matches. Passing by on my bicycle in summer, I would spy them there, clustered in small groups, talking—frightening and fascinating men—some wearing Texas

leisure: free time for rest or recreation

wealth: a lot of money

terra-cotta: brown-red

tawny: brown-yellow

singes: burns on the surface

slam: shut with force and noise

scorn: (the expression of) a feeling of disdain or hate

looks: personal appearance

paradoxically: surprisingly, contradictorily

in awe: with respect and fear

---

*Spanish for "little Negro."
†Latin-American term for "North Americans."

*sombreros** and T-shirts which shone fluorescent in the twilight. I would sit forward in the back seat of our family's '48 Chevy to see them, working alongside Valley highways: dark men on an even horizon, loading a truck amid rows of straight green. Powerful, powerless men. Their fascinating darkness—like mine—to be feared.)

4   "You'll end up looking just like them."

5   Regarding my family, I see faces that do not closely resemble my own. Like some other Mexican families, my family suggests Mexico's confused colonial past. Gathered around a table, we appear to be from separate continents. My father's face recalls faces I have seen in France. His complexion is white—he does not tan;° he does not burn. Over the years, his dark wavy hair has grayed handsomely. But with time his face has sagged° to a perpetual° sigh.° My mother, whose surname is inexplicably° Irish—Moran—has an olive complexion. People have frequently wondered if, perhaps, she is Italian or Portuguese. And, in fact, she looks as though she could be from southern Europe. My mother's face has not aged as quickly as the rest of her body; it remains smooth and glowing—a cool tan—which her gray hair cleanly accentuates.° My older brother has inherited her good looks. When he was a boy people would tell him that he looked like Mario Lanza,† and hearing it he would smile with dimpled° assurance.° He would come home from high school with girl friends who seemed to me glamorous° (because they were) blonds. And during those years I envied him his skin that burned red and peeled like the skin of the *gringos*. His complexion never darkened like mine. My youngest sister is exotically pale, almost ashen.° She is delicately featured, Near Eastern, people have said. Only my older sister has a complexion as dark as mine, though her facial features are much less harshly defined than my own. To many people meeting her, she seems (they say) Polynesian. I am the only one in the family whose face is severely cut to the line of ancient° Indian ancestors.° My face is mournfully long, in the classical Indian manner; my profile suggests one of those beak-nosed Mayan sculptures—the eaglelike face upturned, open-mouthed, against the deserted, primitive sky.

6   "We are Mexicans," my mother and father would say, and taught their four children to say whenever we (often) were asked about

tan: become brown from the sun

sagged: weakened and fallen

perpetual: continual, constant

sigh: a slow, sad breath

inexplicably: in a way that cannot be understood

accentuates: emphasizes

dimpled: from *dimple*, which is a small indentation in the cheek

assurance: confidence

glamorous: fascinating, very attractive

ashen: white, like ashes

ancient: very very old

ancestors: people from whom one is descended (grandparents, etc.)

---

*Spanish for "large hats with brims."
†A handsome singer, popular in the 1950s.

our ancestry. My mother and father scorned° those "white" Mexican-Americans who tried to pass themselves off as Spanish. My parents would never have thought of denying their ancestry. I never denied it: My ancestry is Mexican, I told strangers mechanically. But I never forgot that only my older sister's complexion was as dark as mine.

7   My older sister never spoke to me about her complexion when she was a girl. But I guessed that she found her dark skin a burden.° I knew that she suffered for being [dark]. As she came home from grammar school, little boys came up behind her and pushed her down to the sidewalk. In high school, she struggled in the adolescent° competition for boyfriends in a world of football games and proms,° a world where her looks were plainly uncommon. In college, she was afraid and scornful when dark-skinned foreign students from countries like Turkey and India found her attractive. She revealed her fear of dark skin to me only in adulthood when, regarding her own three children, she quietly admitted relief that they were all light.

8   That is the kind of remark women in my family have often made before. As a boy, I'd stay in the kitchen (never seeming to attract any notice), listening while my aunts spoke of their pleasure at having light children. (The men, some of whom were dark-skinned from years of working out of doors, would be in another part of the house.) It was the woman's spoken concern: the fear of having a dark-skinned son or daughter. Remedies° were exchanged. One aunt prescribed to her sisters the elixir° of large doses of castor oil during the last weeks of pregnancy. (The remedy risked an abortion.°) Children born dark grew up to have their faces treated regularly with a mixture of egg white and lemon juice concentrate. (In my case, the solution never would take.) One Mexican-American friend of my mother's, who regarded it a special blessing° that she had a measure of English blood, spoke disparagingly° of her husband, a construction worker, for being so dark. "He doesn't take care of himself," she complained. But the remark, I noticed, annoyed my mother, who sat tracing an invisible design with her finger on the tablecloth.

9   There was affection too and a kind of humor about these matters. With daring tenderness, one of my uncles would refer to his wife as *mi negra.** An aunt regularly called her dark child *mi feito* (my

scorned: rejected as inferior, hateful

burden: something that is difficult to carry or bear

adolescent: teenage

proms: dances given at high schools

remedies: medicines that heal

elixir: a magical remedy

abortion: miscarriage of a fetus

blessing: something that gives happiness

disparagingly: with disrespect

*Spanish for "my Negro woman."

little ugly one), her smile only partially hidden as she bent down to dig her mouth under his ticklish chin. And at times relatives spoke scornfully of pale, white skin. A *gringo*'s skin resembled *masa*—baker's dough°—someone remarked. Everyone laughed. Voices chuckled° over the fact that the *gringos* spent so many hours in summer sunning themselves. ("They need to get sun because they look like *los muertos*.")*

10   I heard the laughing but remembered what the women had said, with unsmiling voices, concerning dark skin. Nothing I heard outside the house, regarding my skin, was so impressive to me.

11   In public I occasionally heard racial slurs.° Complete strangers would yell out at me. A teenager drove past, shouting, "Hey, Greaser! Hey, Pancho!"° Over his shoulder I saw the giggling° face of his girl friend. A boy pedaled by and announced matter-of-factly, "I pee° on dirty Mexicans." Such remarks would be said so casually that I wouldn't quickly realize that they were being addressed to me. When I did, I would be paralyzed° with embarrassment, unable to return the insult.° (Those times I happened to be with white grammar school friends, *they* shouted back. Imbued with° the mysterious kindness of children, my friends would never ask later why I hadn't yelled out° in my own defense.)

12   In all, there could not have been more than a dozen incidents of name-calling.° That there were so few suggests that I was not a primary victim of racial abuse. But that, even today, I can clearly remember particular incidents is proof of their impact. Because of such incidents, I listened when my parents remarked that Mexicans were often mistreated in California border towns. And in Texas. I listened carefully when I heard that two of my cousins had been refused admittance to an "all-white" swimming pool. And that an uncle had been told by some man to go back to Africa. I followed the progress of the southern black civil rights movement, which was gaining prominent notice in Sacramento's afternoon newspaper. But what most intrigued me was the connection between dark skin and poverty. Because I heard my mother speak so often about the relegation of dark people to menial labor,° I considered the great victims of racism to be those who were poor and forced to do menial work. People like the farmworkers whose skin was dark from the sun.

dough: a mixture of flour and liquid for baking bread

chuckled: laughed softly

racial slurs: cruel remarks based on someone's skin color

Greaser; Pancho: rude names for "Mexican"

giggling: laughing

pee: urinate (slang)

paralyzed: unable to move

insult: a cruel remark

Imbued with: filled with

yelled out: screamed

name-calling: use of cruel names or language

menial labor: hard physical work

---

*Spanish for "the dead."

13   After meeting a black grammar school friend of my sister's, I remember thinking that she wasn't really "black." What interested me was the fact that she wasn't poor. (Her well-dressed parents would come by after work to pick her up in a shiny green Oldsmobile.) By contrast, the garbage men who appeared every Friday morning seemed to me unmistakably black. (I didn't bother to ask my parents why Sacramento garbage men always were black. I thought I knew.) One morning I was in the backyard when a man opened the gate. He was an ugly, square-faced black man with popping red eyes, a pail slung over his shoulder. As he approached, I stood up. And in a voice that seemed to me very weak, I piped,° "Hi." But the man paid me no heed.° He strode past to the can by the garage. In a single broad movement, he overturned its contents into his larger pail. Our can came crashing down as he turned and left me watching, in awe.

piped: said in a high voice

paid me no heed: paid no attention to me

14   "*Pobres negros*,"* my mother remarked when she'd notice a headline in the paper about a civil rights demonstration in the South. "How the *gringos* mistreat° them." In the same tone of voice she'd tell me about the mistreatment her brother endured years before. (After my grandfather's death, my grandmother had come to America with her son and five daughters.) "My sisters, we were still all just teenagers. And since *mi pápa* was dead, my brother had to be the head of the family. He had to support us, to find work. But what skills did he have! Twenty years old. *Pobre.*† He was tall, like your grandfather. And strong. He did construction work. 'Construction!' The *gringos* kept him digging all day, doing the dirtiest jobs. And they would pay him next to nothing. Sometimes they promised him one salary and paid him less when he finished. But what could he do? Report them? We weren't citizens then. He didn't even know English. And he was dark. What chances could he have? As soon as we sisters got older, he went right back to Mexico. He hated this country. He looked so tired when he left. Already with a hunchback.° Still in his twenties. But old-looking. No life for him here. *Pobre.*" ◆

mistreat: act badly towards

hunchback: a curved, deformed back

---

*Spanish for "poor Negroes."
†Spanish for "poor thing."

3. Focused Reading

What experiences and events taught young Richard about discrimination based on skin color and race? As you reread, list the examples he gives.

1. His mother got angry when his skin tanned.

2. _____

3. _____

4. _____

5. _____

6. _____

(7.) _____

(8.) _____

Discuss your list with a small group. Are your lists similar? Have any of you seen or experienced what young Richard did?

4. Analyze the Story

In groups, choose one of the following to discuss. Elect a group member to report your conclusions to the class.

A. What conclusions can you draw about young Richard? What is he like? (Talkative, quiet, aggressive, sensitive, observant?) What parts of the text support these conclusions?

B. Do these pages make you want to read more from *Hunger of Memory*? Why or why not?

READING STRATEGY

Good readers read "between the lines" and draw their own conclusions when they read. They can support these conclusions with evidence from the text.

5. Look at Language

A. You know that **would** is used in polite requests. **(Would you lend me a pen, please?)** and in conditional sentences **(If I had time, I would stay.)**. But **would** can also indicate a past habit, similar to **used to.** The writer uses this form often in the text.

In paragraphs 2–6 of the text, underline all uses of **would** *(or* **'d***) that indicate a past habit.*

B. In constructing a paragraph, writers often put the main (or general) idea of the paragraph at the beginning, in one or more sentences. The main idea is followed by supporting points and examples.

In the following paragraph from the text, underline the sentence(s) containing the main idea. How many supporting points does the author give?

> My older sister never spoke to me about her complexion when she was a girl. But I guessed that she found her dark skin a burden. I knew that she suffered for being [dark]. As she came home from grammar school, little boys came up behind her and pushed her down to the sidewalk. In high school, she struggled in the adolescent competition for boyfriends in a world of football games and proms, a world where her looks were plainly uncommon. In college, she was afraid and scornful when dark-skinned foreign students from countries like Turkey and India found her attractive. She revealed her fear of dark skin to me only in adulthood when, regarding her own three children, she quietly admitted relief that they were all light.

Now look at paragraph 5 in the text. Underline the sentence(s) containing the main idea. How does the writer support this main idea? Count the number of major supporting points he uses.

C. The words in **bold** are color-related verbs.

> I do not **redden** in sunlight. (paragraph 1)
>
> When I was a boy the white summer sun of Sacramento would **darken** me. . . . (paragraph 2)
>
> My father's . . . complexion is white—he does not **tan;** he does not burn. Over the years, his dark wavy hair **has grayed** handsomely. (paragraph 5)

Color-related verbs are formed as follows from adjectives. The verbs can mean either "become (a color)" or "cause to become (a color)."

Adjective	Verb	Adjective	Verb
red	redden	tan	tan
white	whiten	gray	gray
black	blacken	yellow	yellow
dark	darken	brown	brown
light	lighten		

Fill in the blanks with one of the verbs above. Use the correct tense.

1. Richard's mother did not like him to _____ in the sun.

2. She tried to _____ his skin with a mixture of egg white and lemon juice concentrate.

3. Richard envied his handsome brother because his skin _____ in the sun.

4. Both of Richard's parents' hair had _____.

NOTE: Many other adjectives form verbs by adding the suffix *-en*. Below are some examples.

soft—soften	sad—sadden
hard—harden	glad—gladden
flat—flatten	neat—neaten
sweet—sweeten	wide—widen
sharp—sharpen	deep—deepen

6. Move Beyond the Story

Discussion

A. Imagine you are an international group of community leaders. You have received one million dollars from the United Nations to work on solving the problem of racial, religious, and/or ethnic discrimination around the world. How will you spend the money? Write a concrete proposal.

B. Do all groups of people in your country enjoy the same rights and freedoms? Describe the situation in your country. How are your country's problems with discrimination and injustice similar to those in the United States? How are they different?

Writing

A. In paragraph 5 of the text, Mr. Rodriguez gives a physical description of his family. Write something similar about your family.

B. Young Richard was a victim of insults and name-calling. Have you ever experienced anything similar? What happened? How did it make you feel at the time? How does it make you feel now? Write a letter to the person who insulted you telling your side of the story.

Meet the Author

HISAYE YAMAMOTO *(born 1920)*

HISAYE YAMAMOTO was born to Japanese immigrant parents in California. During World War II, when the United States was at war with Japan, the author and her family were put in a concentration camp in Arizona, along with 110,000 other Americans of Japanese origin. Ms. Yamamoto's 1988 collection of stories, *Seventeen Syllables and Other Stories*, focuses on the lives of Japanese-American women both in and out of World War II concentration camps. The following story comes from this collection.

Ms. Yamamoto lives in Los Angeles, California.

1. Anticipate the Story

Story Summary

The events in this story are simple and few. The year is 1950. Esther Kuroiwa, a Japanese-American woman, is taking a bus in Los Angeles to visit her husband in the hospital. A loud-mouthed drunk gets on the bus, followed by an elderly Chinese couple. The drunk begins to speak loud, ugly words to the couple. By the time Esther arrives at the hospital, she feels so helpless and sick that she can't stop crying.

Historical Background

Although the story events are simple, Esther's psychological reactions to them are complex. To understand her reactions fully, you need to know that Japanese Americans were targets of intense discrimination in the United States during World War II because the United States was at war with Japan. Many Japanese Americans, like Esther, were put in concentration camps. In 1950, the year this story was written, the United States was at war with North Korea, which was militarily supported by China. One result was increased discrimination against people of Chinese origin in the United States.

> **READING STRATEGY**
>
> Read a difficult text the first time for the general idea. Use the context to get the meaning of some new words. Remember, you don't need to know every word to get the general idea.

2. Global Reading

Read the story the first time to get the general idea. Don't be concerned if you don't understand all the details.

Jot down your reactions or questions about the story here or in your journal. Share them with a partner or group.

reader response

Wilshire Bus

◆◆

Hisaye Yamamoto

WILSHIRE BOULEVARD BEGINS SOMEWHERE near the heart of downtown Los Angeles and, except for a few digressions scarcely worth mentioning, goes straight out to the edge of the Pacific Ocean. It is a wide boulevard and traffic on it is fairly fast. For the most part, it is bordered on either side with examples of the recent stark architecture which favors a great deal of glass. As the boulevard approaches the sea, however, the landscape becomes a bit more pastoral,° so that the university and the soldiers' home there give the appearance of being huge country estates.

pastoral: rural, natural

2   Esther Kuroiwa got to know this stretch of territory quite well while her husband Buro was in one of the hospitals at the soldiers' home. They had been married less than a year when his back, injured in the war, began troubling him again, and he was forced to take three months of treatments at Sawtelle before he was able to go back to work. During this time, Esther was permitted to visit him twice a week and she usually took the yellow bus out on Wednesdays because she did not know the first thing about driving and because her friends were not able to take her except on Sundays. She always enjoyed the long bus ride very much because her seat companions usually turned out to be amiable,° and if they did not, she took vicarious pleasure° in gazing out at° the almost unmitigated° elegance along the fabulous street.

amiable: friendly

vicarious pleasure: pleasure enjoyed by imaginary participation

gazing at: looking at

unmitigated: absolute

3   It was on one of these Wednesday trips that Esther committed a grave° sin of omission° which caused her later to burst into tears and which caused her acute discomfort for a long time afterwards whenever something reminded her of it.

grave: very serious

sin of omission: failure to do something one should have done

4   The man came on the bus quite early and Esther noticed him briefly as he entered because he said gaily to the driver, "You robber. All you guys do is take money from me every day, just for giving me a short lift!"

5   Handsome in a red-faced way, greying, medium of height, and dressed in a dark grey sport suit with a yellow-and-black flowered shirt, he said this in a nice, resonant, carrying voice which got the response of a scattering of titters° from the bus. Esther, somewhat amused and

titters: nervous laughs

classifying him as a somatotonic,° promptly forgot about him. And since she was sitting alone in the first regular seat, facing the back of the driver and the two front benches facing each other, she returned to looking out the window.

6   At the next stop, a considerable mass of people piled on and the last two climbing up were an elderly Oriental man and his wife. Both were neatly and somberly clothed and the woman, who wore her hair in a bun and carried a bunch of yellow and dark red chrysanthemums,° came to sit with Esther. Esther turned her head to smile a greeting (well, here we are, Orientals together on a bus), but the woman was watching, with some concern, her husband who was asking directions of the driver.

7   His faint English was inflected in such a way as to make Esther decide he was probably Chinese, and she noted that he had to repeat his question several times before the driver could answer it. Then he came to sit in the seat across the aisle from his wife. It was about then that a man's voice, which Esther recognized soon as belonging to the somatotonic, began a loud monologue° in the seat just behind her. It was not really a monologue, since he seemed to be addressing his seat companion, but this person was not heard to give a single answer. The man's subject was a figure in the local sporting world who had a nice fortune invested in several of the shining buildings the bus was just passing.

8   "He's as tight-fisted° as they make them, as tight-fisted as they come," the man said. "Why, he wouldn't give you the sweat of his . . ." He paused here to rephrase his metaphor, ". . . wouldn't give you the sweat° off his palm!"

9   And he continued in this vein, discussing the private life of the famous man so frankly that Esther knew he must be quite drunk. But she listened with interest, wondering how much of this diatribe° was true, because the public legend about the famous man was emphatic about his charity.° Suddenly, the woman with the chrysanthemums jerked around to get a look at the speaker and Esther felt her giving him a quick but thorough examination before she turned back around.

10   "So you don't like it?" the man inquired, and it was a moment before Esther realized that he was now directing his attention to her seat neighbor.

somatotonic: an aggressive, oversocial person

chrysanthemums: showy, ball-shaped flowers

monologue: a long speech by one person

tight-fisted: stingy, not wanting to spend money (idiomatic)

sweat: the moisture that comes through the skin

diatribe: abusive, hostile criticism

charity: acts of goodwill, the giving of money

11   "Well, if you don't like it," he continued, "why don't you get off this bus, why don't you go back where you came from? Why don't you go back to China?"

12   Then, his voice growing jovial,° as though he were certain of the support of the bus in this at least, he embroidered on this theme with a new eloquence, "Why don't you go back to China, where you can be coolies° working in your bare feet out in the rice fields? You can let your pigtails° grow and grow in China. Alla samee, mama, no tickee no shirtee. Ha, pretty good, no tickee no shirtee!"*

13   He chortled with delight and seemed to be looking around the bus for approval. Then some memory caused him to launch on a new idea "Or why don't you go back to Trinidad? They got Chinks° running the whole she-bang° in Trinidad. Every place you go in Trinidad . . ."

14   As he talked on, Esther, pretending to look out the window, felt the tenseness in the body of the woman beside her. The only movement from her was the trembling of the chrysanthemums with the motion of the bus. Without turning her head, Esther was also aware that a man, a mild-looking man with thinning hair and glasses, on one of the front benches was smiling at the woman and shaking his head mournfully in sympathy, but she doubted whether the woman saw.

15   Esther herself, while believing herself properly annoyed° with the speaker and sorry for the old couple, felt quite detached.° She found herself wondering whether the man meant her in his exclusion order° or whether she was identifiably Japanese. Of course, he was not sober enough to be interested in such fine distinctions, but it did matter, she decided, because she was Japanese, not Chinese, and therefore in the present case immune.° Then she was startled to realize that what she was actually doing was gloating over° the fact that the drunken man had specified the Chinese as the unwanted.

16   Briefly, there bobbled on her memory the face of an elderly Oriental man whom she had once seen from a streetcar on her way home from work. (This was not long after she had returned to Los Angeles from the concentration camp in Arkansas and been lucky enough to get a clerical job with the Community Chest.) The old man was on a concrete island at Seventh and Broadway, waiting for his streetcar. She had looked down on him benignly° as a fellow Oriental,

jovial: full of good humor

coolies: in Asia, unskilled laborers

pigtails: long braids of hair

Chinks: racist term for Chinese

the whole she-bang: everything (slang)

annoyed: irritated, bothered

detached: not involved, separate

exclusion order: a system of excluding some people

immune: protected against something harmful

gloating over: looking on with pleasure

benignly: kindly

*The man is imitating the way he thinks Chinese people speak.

from her seat by the window, then been suddenly thrown for a loop°
by the legend on a large lapel button on his jacket. I AM KOREAN, said
the button.

17   Heat suddenly rising to her throat, she had felt angry, then
desolate° and betrayed.° True, reason had returned to ask whether she
might not, under the circumstances, have worn such a button herself.
She had heard rumors of I AM CHINESE buttons. So it was true then;
why not I AM KOREAN buttons, too? Wryly, she wished for an I AM
JAPANESE button, just to be able to call the man's attention to it, "Look
at me!" But perhaps the man didn't even read English, perhaps he had
been actually threatened, perhaps it was not his doing—his solicitous
children perhaps had urged him to wear the badge.

18   Trying now to make up for her moral shabbiness,° she turned
towards the little woman and smiled at her across the chrysanthemums,
shaking her head a little to get across her message (don't pay any
attention to that stupid old drunk, he doesn't know what he's saying,
let's take things like this in our stride). But the woman, in turn looking
at her, presented a face so impassive yet cold, and eyes so
expressionless yet hostile, that Esther's overture° fell quite flat.°

19   Okay, okay, if that's the way you feel about it, she thought to
herself. Then the bus made another stop and she heard the man
proclaim ringingly, "So clear out,° all of you, and remember to take
every last one of your slant-eyed° pickaninnies° with you!" This was his
final advice as he stepped down from the middle door. The bus
remained at the stop long enough for Esther to watch the man cross the
street with a slightly exploring step. Then, as it started up again, the
bespectacled man in front stood up to go and made a clumsy speech to
the Chinese couple and possibly to Esther. "I want you to know," he
said, "that we aren't all like that man. We don't all feel the way he does.
We believe in an America that is a melting pot of all sorts of people. I'm
originally Scotch and French myself." With that, he came over and
shook the hand of the Chinese man.

20   "And you, young lady," he said to the girl behind Esther, "you
deserve a Purple Heart* or something for having to put up with that
sitting beside you."

---

*A medal of merit given by the U.S. military.

thrown for a loop: surprised and confused (idiomatic)

desolate: alone, abandoned

betrayed: deceived

moral shabbiness: disgraceful, shameful behavior or character

overture: an indication of a willingness to speak

fell . . . flat: failed

clear out: get out (colloquial)

slant-eyed: racist description of Asian eyes

pickaninnies: racist word for *children*

21   Then he, too, got off.

22   The rest of the ride was uneventful and Esther stared out the window with eyes that did not see. Getting off at last at the soldiers' home, she was aware of the Chinese couple getting off after her, but she avoided looking at them. Then, while she was walking towards Buro's hospital very quickly, there arose in her mind some words she had once read and let stick in her craw:° People say, do not regard what he says, now he is in liquor.° Perhaps it is the only time he ought to be regarded.

23   These words repeated themselves until her saving detachment was gone every bit and she was filled once again in her life with the infuriatingly helpless, insidiously° sickening° sensation° of there being in the world nothing solid she could put her finger on, nothing solid she could come to grips with,° nothing solid she could sink her teeth into,° nothing solid.

24   When she reached Buro's room and caught sight of his welcoming face, she ran to his bed and broke into sobs that she could not control. Buro was amazed because it was hardly her first visit and she had never shown such weakness before, but solving the mystery handily, he patted her head, looked around smugly at his roommates, and asked tenderly, "What's the matter? You've been missing me a whole lot, huh?" And she, finally drying her eyes, sniffed and nodded and bravely smiled and answered him with the question, yes, weren't women silly? ◆

let stick in her craw: not accepted (idiomatic)

in liquor: drunk

insidiously: slowly and dangerously

sickening: disgusting

sensation: feeling

come to grips with: try to manage with (idiomatic)

sink her teeth into: hold onto (idiomatic)

3. Focused Reading

As you reread the story, think about the changes in Esther's psychological state. In the following table write how she feels at each stage of the story. Choose from the adjectives in the box, or use others you find in the story.

Story Events	How Esther Feels
Esther's trip begins A drunk man gets on the bus	Calm and enthusiastic about trip
The drunk man loudly discusses a rich man in the local sporting world	
The drunk man addresses the elderly Chinese couple	
FLASHBACK: Esther remembers a man she once saw who was wearing an "I AM KOREAN" button	
Esther smiles at the Chinese woman	
Esther gets off the bus and goes to the hospital	

ADJECTIVES
amused
angry
annoyed
anxious
betrayed
calm
curious
detached
enthusiastic
guilty
helpless
interested
irritated
sick
superior
sympathetic

Discuss your answers with a group. What happened on the bus to make Esther's feelings change so much?

4. Analyze the Story

In groups, choose one of the following to discuss. Elect a group member to report your conclusions to the class.

A. In paragraph 3 we read, "It was on one of these Wednesday trips that Esther committed a grave sin of omission. . . ." In your opinion, what was this sin of omission?

B. How did Esther and the rest of the people on the bus react to the drunken man's words (paragraphs 11–13)? How would you have reacted?

C. Try to summarize the main idea(s) of the story in two or three sentences. Write your summary.

5. Look at Language

You know that **but** *links two ideas that are in* **contrast.** *Study the following example from the text.*

> Getting off at last at the soldiers' home, (Esther) was aware of the Chinese couple getting off after her, **but** she avoided looking at them. (paragraph 22)

A. *Now circle other markers of contrast in the examples from the text. Try to rephrase the ideas using* **but.**

1. "Esther herself, while believing herself properly annoyed with the speaker and sorry for the old couple, felt quite detached." (paragraph 15)

2. "For the most part, [Wilshire Boulevard] is bordered on either side with examples of the recent stark architecture which favors a great deal of glass. As the boulevard approaches the sea, however, the landscape becomes a bit more pastoral. . . ." (paragraph 1)

3. "Trying now to make up for her moral shabbiness, [Esther] turned towards the little woman and smiled at her. . . . But the woman, in turn looking at her, presented a face so impassive yet cold, and eyes so expressionless yet hostile, that Esther's overture fell quite flat." (paragraph 18)

B. *Did you find three markers of contrast in addition to* **but***? Write them here.*

_____

_____

_____

C. *Below are other examples of contrast markers. Circle them. Try to rephrase the ideas using* but.

1. Whereas English uses the Latin alphabet, Russian uses the Cyrillic.

2. I'm extremely busy. I have time to go to the movies, though.

3. He said he enjoyed the party when in fact he found it boring.

4. She decided to accept the job because although the salary is low, the benefits are excellent.

5. The boss doesn't know whether to fire our new employee or not. He is neither punctual nor friendly. On the other hand, he's very productive.

6. Move Beyond the Story

Discussion

A. This story raises the question of what people should do when they witness abuse or discrimination. Working in groups, try to reach a *consensus* (agreement) about what to do in the following situations.

1. You are a passenger on a bus and you hear a drunk man sitting near you make abusive racial remarks to another passenger.

2. A very good friend of yours, in passing, makes a negative comment about a racial or ethnic group: "Oh, you know those _____, they're stupid/dirty/dishonest."

B. Esther did not tell her husband the truth about why she was crying. Imagine that she had told the truth. Role-play the scene between Esther and her husband.

Writing

A. Have you ever been in a situation like Esther's? Describe the situation and your reaction.

B. Have you ever been a victim of racial abuse or discrimination? Write about what happened.

UNIT 6 ♦ *Review*

♦♦

Texts	Some of the Characters
COMPLEXION	young Richard Richard's mother Richard's dark-skinned sister the people who shouted racial slurs at Richard
WILSHIRE BUS	Esther the old Chinese couple the man wearing the "I AM KOREAN" button the drunk man the man with glasses on the bus

Work individually, with a partner, or with a group to complete one of these tasks.

1. Rank some or all of the above characters on this scale. Who is the most tolerant and nonracist? Who is the least tolerant? Who is somewhere in between? Explain your ranking.

tolerant and
nonracist

intolerant
and racist

2. Compare the two stories. Can you find at least three similarities?

Appendixes

WORLD MAP

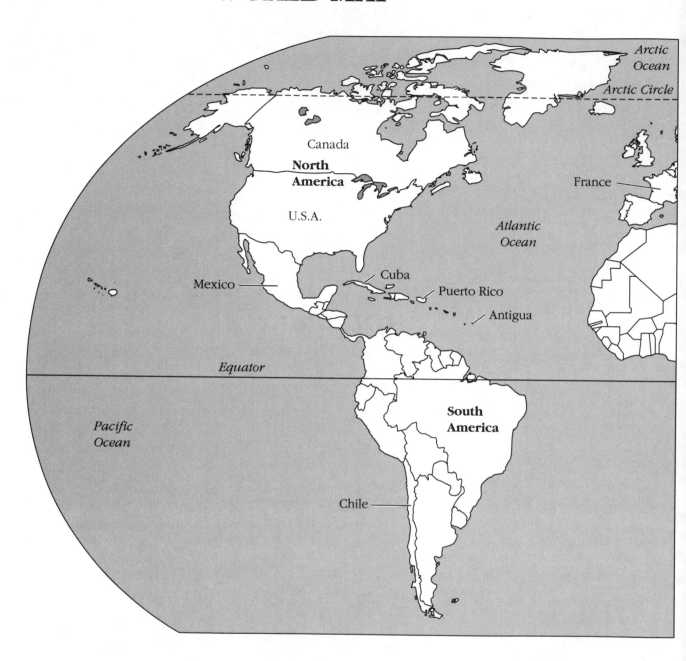

Arctic
Ocean

Arctic Circle

Canada

**North
America**

France

U.S.A.

Atlantic
Ocean

Mexico

Cuba

Puerto Rico

Antigua

Equator

**South
America**

Pacific
Ocean

Chile

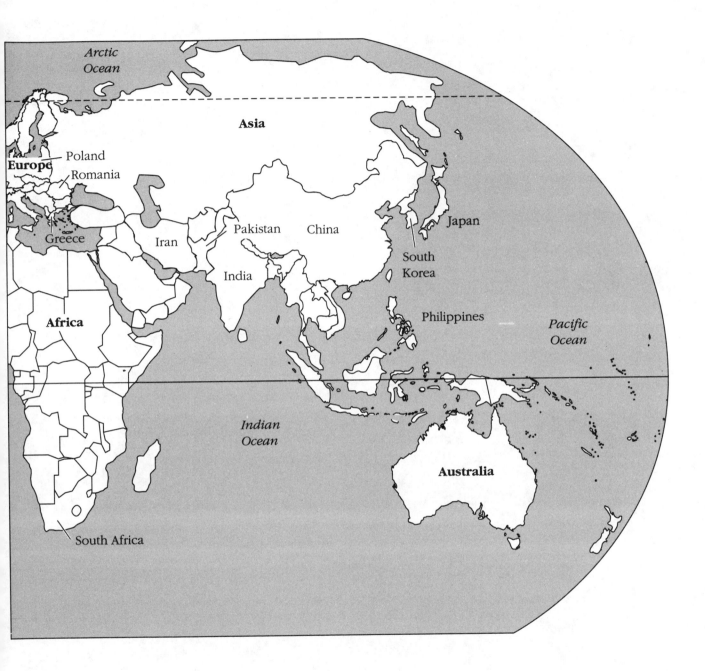

Arctic
Ocean

Asia

Europe

Poland

Romania

Greece

Iran

Pakistan

India

China

Japan

South
Korea

Philippines

Africa

Pacific
Ocean

Indian
Ocean

Australia

South Africa

OTHER SELECTED WORKS
BY AUTHORS IN THIS VOLUME

Virginia Cerenio
Trespassing Innocence (1989)

Sandra Cisneros
My Wicked Wicked Ways (1987)
Woman Hollering Creek (1991)
Loose Woman (1994)

Andrei Codrescu
Monsieur Teste in America (1988)
The Hole in the Flag: A Romanian Exile's Story of Return and Revolution (1991)
Road Scholar (1993)

Judith Ortiz Cofer
Terms of Survival (1987)
Reaching for the Mainland (1987)
The Line of the Sun (1989)

Victor Hernandez Cruz
Snaps (1969)
Tropicalization (1976)
Rhythm Content and Flavor (1989)
Red Beans (1991)

Oscar Hijuelos
The Mambo Kings Play Songs of Love (1990)

Eva Hoffman
Exit into History: A Journey through Eastern Europe (1993)

Kim Yong Ik
The Happy Days (1960)
The Diving Gourd (1962)
Wedding Shoes (1984)

Jamaica Kincaid
At the Bottom of the River (1984)
Annie John (1985)
A Small Place (1988)
Autobiography of My Mother (1994)

Mark Mathabane
Kaffir Boy (1984)
Love in Black and White (1992)

Pat Mora
Borders (1986)
Communion (1991)
Pablo's Tree (1994)
Ana Meets the Wind (1995)

Bharati Mukherjee
Days and Nights in Calcutta (1977)
The Middleman and Other Stories (1988)
Jasmine (1989)

Nahid Rachlin
Foreigner (1978)
Married to a Stranger (1983)
Veils (1992)

Richard Rodriguez
Days of Obligation: An Argument with My Mexican Father (1992)

Amy Tan
The Kitchen God's Wife (1991)

Liu Zongren
Tanyin Alley (1994)

CREDITS

Text

Grateful acknowledgment is given to the following publishing companies and individuals for permission to print, reprint, or adapt materials for which they own copyrights:

Arriving

"Exile" from *Lost in Translation* by Eva Hoffman. Copyright © 1989 by Eva Hoffman. Used by permission of Dutton Signet, a division of Penguin Books USA Inc.

"Visitors, 1965" from *Our House in the Last World* by Oscar Hijuelos. Copyright © 1983 by Oscar Hijuelos. Reprinted by permission of Persea Books.

"Poor Visitor" from *Lucy* by Jamaica Kincaid. Copyright © 1990 by Jamaica Kincaid. Reprinted by permission of Farrar, Straus & Giroux, Inc.

Learning English

"Elena," by Pat Mora, is reprinted by permission of the publisher from *Chants* (Houston: Arte Público Press, University of Houston, 1985).

"Languages," from *A Craving for Swan* by Andrei Codrescu, is reprinted by permission. © 1986 by the Ohio State University Press. All rights reserved.

"A Book-Writing Venture," by Kim Yong Ik, is reprinted by permission of the author.

Feeling Homesick

"No Speak English," by Sandra Cisneros from *The House on Mango Street*. Copyright © 1984 by Sandra Cisneros. Published in the United States by Vintage Books, a division of Random House, Inc., New York, and distributed in Canada by Random House of Canada Limited, Toronto. Reprinted by permission of Susan Bergholz Literary Services, New York.

Excerpt from **Two Years in the Melting Pot,** by Liu Zongren. Reprinted by permission of China Books & Periodicals, Inc.

Excerpt from **Wife** by Bharati Mukherjee, Fawcett Books. Copyright © 1975 by Bharati Mukherjee, reprinted 1992. Reprinted by permission of The Elaine Markson Literary Agency, Inc.

Changing

"Family Photos: Black and White: 1960," by Virginia Cerenio, was first published in *The Forbidden Stitch: An Asian-American Women's Anthology*, edited by Shirley Geok-lin Lim et al., published by Calyx Books © 1989. Reprinted by permission of the editors and publisher.

"The Man Who Came to the Last Floor" from *Mainland* by Victor Hernandez Cruz. Copyright © 1973 by Victor Hernandez Cruz. Reprinted by permission of Random House, Inc.

"Vida," by Judith Ortiz Cofer, is reprinted with permission of the publisher from *Silent Dancing: A Partial Remembrance of a Puerto Rican Childhood* (Houston: Arte Público Press, University of Houston, 1990).

Intersecting Cultures

Excerpt from **Kaffir Boy in America** by Mark Mathabane. Reprinted with the permission of Charles Scribner's Sons, an imprint of Macmillan Publishing Company. Copyright © 1989 Mark Mathabane.

Excerpt from **"Four Directions,"** from *The Joy Luck Club* by Amy Tan. Reprinted by permission of The Putnam Publishing Group. Copyright © 1989 by Amy Tan.

"A Clean Break," by Tahira Naqvi, printed by permission of the author.

"Journey of Love" by Nahid Rachlin. Reprinted by permission of Gina Maccoby Literary Agency. Copyright © 1988 by Nahid Rachlin.

Facing Discrimination

"Complexion" from *Hunger of Memory* by Richard Rodriguez. Copyright © 1982 by Richard Rodriguez. Reprinted by permission of David R. Godine, Publisher.

"Wilshire Bus" from *Seventeen Syllables* by Hisaye Yamamoto. Copyright © 1988 by Kitchen Table: Women of Color Press and Hisaye Yamamoto. Used by permission of the author and Kitchen Table: Women of Color Press, P.O. Box 906, Latham, NY 12110.

Photo

Grateful acknowledgment is given to the following for providing photographs:

p. 1   FPG/Jay Lurie

p. 2   Dutton Signet, a division of Penguin Books USA Inc.

p. 10   Persea Books

p. 17   © 1990 Sigrid Estrada

p. 25   © Ken Light

p. 26   Arte Público

p. 32   S. F. Tabachnikoff

p. 40   Jeff Machlin

p. 51   FPG/Frank Saragnese

p. 52   Ruben Guzman

p. 59   China Books & Periodicals Inc.

p. 67   Tony Colby

p. 79   FPG/Buddy Mays

p. 80   Virginia Cerenio

p. 87   Victor Hernandez Cruz

p. 99   Arte Público

p. 111   FPG/David McGlynn

p. 112   Charles Scribner's Sons, an imprint of Macmillan Publishing Company

p. 121   Robert Foot Horap

p. 129   Tahira Naqvi

p. 139   Howard Rachlin

p. 155   FPG/Telegraph Colour Library

p. 156   George Borchardt

p. 167   © Marilyn Sanders

INDEX

Y